By Sarah Machajewski

Portions of this book originally appeared in *Political Corruption* by Debra A. Miller.

LUCENT
PRESS

Published in 2019 by
Lucent Press, an Imprint of Greenhaven Publishing, LLC
353 3rd Avenue
Suite 255
New York, NY 10010

Designer: Deanna Paternostro
Editor: Jennifer Lombardo

Cataloging-in-Publication Data

Names: Machajewski, Sarah.
Title: Political corruption and the abuse of power / Sarah Machajewski.
Description: New York : Lucent Press, 2019. | Series: Hot topics | Includes index.
Identifiers: ISBN 9781534563438 (pbk.) | ISBN 9781534563414 (library bound) | ISBN 9781534563421 (ebook)
Subjects: LCSH: Political corruption–Juvenile literature. | Political leadership–Moral and ethical aspects–Juvenile literature.
Classification: LCC JF1081.M55 2019 | DDC 364.1'323–dc23

Printed in the United States of America

CPSIA compliance information: Batch #BS18KL: For further information contact Greenhaven Publishing LLC, New York, New York at 1-844-317-7404.

Please visit our website, www.greenhavenpublishing.com. For a free color catalog of all our high-quality books, call toll free 1-844-317-7404 or fax 1-844-317-7405.

CONTENTS

Adolescence is a time when many people begin to take notice of the world around them. News channels, blogs, and talk radio shows are constantly promoting one view or another; very few are unbiased. Young people also hear conflicting information from parents, friends, teachers, and acquaintances. Often, they will hear only one side of an issue or be given flawed information. People who are trying to support a particular viewpoint may cite inaccurate facts and statistics on their blogs, and news programs present many conflicting views of important issues in our society. In a world where it seems everyone has a platform to share their thoughts, it can be difficult to find unbiased, accurate information about important issues.

It is not only facts that are important. In blog posts, in comments on online videos, and on talk shows, people will share opinions that are not necessarily true or false, but can still have a strong impact. For example, many young people struggle with their body image. Seeing or hearing negative comments about particular body types online can have a huge effect on the way someone views himself or herself and may lead to depression and anxiety. Although it is important not to keep information hidden from young people under the guise of protecting them, it is equally important to offer encouragement on issues that affect their mental health.

The titles in the Hot Topics series provide readers with different viewpoints on important issues in today's society. Many of these issues, such as teen pregnancy and Internet safety, are of immediate concern to young people. This series aims to give readers factual context on these crucial topics in a way that lets them form their own opinions. The facts presented throughout also serve to empower readers to help themselves or support people they know who are struggling with many of the challenges adolescents face today. Although negative viewpoints are not ignored or downplayed, this series allows young people to see that the challenges they face are not insurmountable. Eating disorders can be overcome, the Internet can be navigated safely, and pregnant teens do not have to feel hopeless.

Quotes encompassing all viewpoints are presented and cited so readers can trace them back to their original source, verifying for themselves whether the information comes from a reputable place. Additional books and websites are listed, giving readers a starting point from which to continue their own research. Chapter questions encourage discussion, allowing young people to hear and understand their classmates' points of view as they further solidify their own. Full-color photographs and enlightening charts provide a deeper understanding of the topics at hand. All of these features augment the informative text, helping young people understand the world they live in and formulate their own opinions concerning the best way they can improve it.

A Disease Called Corruption

Serious actions such as embezzlement, political favors, kickbacks, and money laundering are all forms of political corruption—a term that includes everything from the occasional acceptance of illegal bribes by government officials to more subtle and systemic, or deeply engrained, types of political influence. Corruption is a well-documented phenomenon in politics, but today it is increasingly becoming a focus of great concern, both in the United States and in nations around the world. In the 21st century, experts view political corruption as one of the biggest challenges facing developed and developing countries, and the attention paid to it is only growing as citizens increasingly move to hold elected officials accountable for their actions.

By tuning into any news program or visiting any news outlet's website, viewers are bound to see highly sensationalized scandals involving important government officials, whether they have actually done something illegal or unethical or are simply facing accusations that their relationship with wealthy corporations is suspicious. Political corruption affects all levels of government and is covered in local, national, and even international news.

For example, political corruption scandals dominated the news in the United States during the 2016 presidential election year. Two names in the news—Donald Trump and Hillary Clinton—were constantly dragged through the mud as accusations of collusion—secret or illegal cooperation for personal gain—with foreign governments and misuse of email servers flew across party lines. This became an even more difficult situation when the little evidence that was available seemed to contradict itself constantly.

Even outside of heated presidential politics, political corruption occurs almost daily across party lines and across all levels of influence. Many experts and commentators say there is a systemic "culture of corruption" in American politics.

One example of this culture of corruption involved longtime California Republican congressman Randy Cunningham. He was a former Navy top gun pilot who had a reputation for patriotism and honesty. However, he used his position on the House Intelligence and Appropriations committees to steer

Presidential candidates Hillary Clinton and Donald Trump were both accused of corruption during and after the 2016 election.

millions of dollars in defense contracts to companies in exchange for $2.4 million in bribes. A bribe is money or high-priced goods illegally paid to someone, generally a political figure, to influence their decisions. In one instance, a contractor bought Cunningham's home in San Diego, California, for more than it was worth and provided him with a 42-foot (13 m) yacht called the *Duke-Stir*. These actions were considered a form of bribery because the contractor was using a legitimate transaction—the sale of the house—to cover the fact that he was paying Cunningham a large amount of money and giving him a gift worth even more money. In return, the contractor received government work. By law, companies are supposed to win contracts by bidding for them. Giving the contractor work without making him go through the bidding process took opportunities away from other companies. Other bribes Cunningham accepted included $1 million in checks, a $200,000 down payment on a condo, and numerous other expensive gifts, such as oriental rugs, a Rolls Royce automobile, and antique furniture. In 2005, Cunningham pled guilty to bribery and tax evasion (refusal to pay taxes). He served an eight-year prison term, which he completed in 2013. The Cunningham scandal illustrates that, even today, clear examples of bribery still exist in U.S. politics.

In another example of corruption, top Republican aide and Washington lobbyist Jack Abramoff pled guilty in 2006 to three criminal felony counts of tax evasion and bribery. In this high-profile lobbying scandal, Abramoff admitted to over-charging Native American tribes around $80 million for lobby-ing activities and providing gifts and trips to public officials in exchange for favors. Campaign reports also revealed hundreds of thousands of dollars in political contributions coming from Abramoff and his clients to prominent legislators. A lobbyist is someone who works either for pay or on a volunteer basis to convince politicians to vote a certain way on issues the lob-byist represents. For instance, a lobbyist for a health insurance company might meet with a congressman to ask them to vote on issues in a way that benefits the company. If the lobbyist is paid for this work, it is by the health insurance company, not by any government official or group. Lobbying is very common and perfectly legal as long as lobbyists use only their words to try to convince a politician to see their point of view. Offering money, gifts, or favors, as Abramoff did, is illegal. Abramoff pled guilty in January 2006 and was sentenced to five years and ten months in prison. Additionally, he was ordered to pay more than $21 million in restitution, or reimbursement, to the people he had cheated out of money. Also convicted in the scandal were Abramoff's former lobbying partner, Michael Scanlon, as well as two former aides of powerful Republican House majority leader Tom DeLay, whom Abramoff worked for. DeLay himself was indicted for illegal campaign finance activities in Texas and re-signed from Congress later that year.

A third name, Ken Lay, represents another type of corrup-tion: corporate fraud. Many critics say this type of corruption happens when government officials "look the other way" when corporations illegally make campaign donations to high-level politicians. Lay was the chief executive officer (CEO) of Enron, a huge energy company that imploded in a bankruptcy scandal that caused the loss of 4,000 jobs as well as millions of dollars' worth of employee pensions. The scandal brought financial ruin to its many investors.

A Justice Department investigation found that Enron executives had lied to everyone—about everything. Through a scheme of deception that lasted for years, executives claimed the company's profits were higher than they actually were and concealed debts while selling off their own personal stock, essentially cheating employees and investors out of money. Years later, following a much-publicized trial, Ken Lay and Jeffrey Skilling were convicted on multiple counts of securities and wire fraud, but Lay died of a heart attack before receiving his sentencing.

While Lay and Skilling were employees of private corporations, many commentators believe a lack of government oversight led to the Enron scandal. History shows that government officials, including those associated with former President George W. Bush's family, helped the company win favorable regulatory conditions and other government benefits in exchange for millions in campaign contributions. These actions allowed Enron officials to gain huge profits and hide the company's financial weaknesses at the expense of consumers and stockholders who had no one in the government to protect them.

The Enron scandal was one of the most highly publicized corruption scandals of the early 2000s. Shown here are some of the people involved testifying before Congress.

An International Problem

Similar instances of outright corruption also trouble other countries, both strong and weak. In developing countries, widespread official corruption often places large amounts of public money into private hands, which reinforces oppression through poverty, disease, and economic underdevelopment. As the world economy moves increasingly toward globalization and countries rely more on each other for trade, corruption has only increased. In many places, public welfare is controlled by an endless parade of unethical and corrupt politicians and corporate executives. This often makes citizens apathetic, or uncaring, about politics; they come to believe that corruption and politics go hand-in-hand and nothing can be done to change it, so there is no point in trying. The result, many experts say, is voter apathy, reflected in shockingly low voter turnouts. When no one votes on issues they care about, nothing changes, which reinforces the idea that there is no point in trying to create change.

In the United States as well as the rest of the world, individuals and organizations have attempted to end corruption in politics. Early U.S. reforms resulted in fewer cases of bribery and similar forms of corruption that once were common. However, a different problem of campaign finance corruption took its place: corruption that involves corporate and special interest money in political campaigns and the buying of political influence. This involves companies trying to get a political candidate to vote in ways that benefit it by paying large amounts of money to support the candidate's campaign. The idea is that the politician will feel like they owe the company a favor for helping them get into office. This is what people mean when they say a politician is "in the pocket of" a particular company or industry. For example, if a politician were said to be "in the pocket of Big Pharma," it means people know or believe pharmaceutical companies have paid to influence the way that politician votes. Some instances of this are legal, while others are illegal; there are certain restrictions on campaign donations, but each attempt to legislate in this area has been complicated with new forms of corrupt behavior.

While the situation seems hopeless, there is a shifting tide of public opposition to corruption on all levels that is reflected in a number of local, national, and international reform movements. With the help of committed leadership, a hard-working press, and continuing political advocacy, the disease of corruption may one day be eliminated from politics.

Understanding Political Corruption

There are many forms of political corruption, each with varying degrees of legal consequences. For instance, someone may accept a $100 bribe or embezzle millions of dollars. However, no matter what form it takes, any kind of political corruption is problematic. It defies the very purpose of a government, which most people agree is to promote and protect the public good. If government officials fall to corruption, they cannot carry out their duty as a representative of the public. Political corruption poses a significant threat to both basic democratic principles and economic development.

What Is Political Corruption?

In the broadest sense, political corruption is the misuse of public or government power for an illegal or improper purpose. The World Bank and the International Monetary Fund (IMF) define it as "the abuse of public office for private gain."[1] Often, the person acting improperly is doing so for some form of private financial gain, such as increasing their personal wealth or their business profits, or to create a less competitive or regulated business environment that might lead to financial gain. If a government official has personal debts through something such as gambling, they may take a bribe or embezzle public funds to pay it off. Sometimes, they may act to simply grow their own personal bank account. Officials have accepted bribes from individuals or corporations in exchange for voting a certain way. Their vote could help the company by discouraging regulations that could harm company profits. Sometimes, bribes cause an elected official to look the other way on what is obviously corporate criminal activity.

Other times, however, money is not the object at all; the goal is simply to gain greater political power or to achieve specific political goals considered important to a particular person or

A Glossary of Corruption

Not everyone is familiar with the terms people use to describe corruption. Below are some of the most common corrupt behaviors people in power engage in.

bribery: Offering someone in power gifts, money, or favors to convince them to do something they are not supposed to do. A bribe is also known as a kickback or payoff.

collusion: Illegally working with a person, organization, or government, especially as a way to cheat others for personal gain.

embezzlement: Stealing money from a person's employer that has been placed in the employee's trust (for instance, a cashier stealing money from the cash register).

extortion: The use of a person's power to threaten someone into providing money, gifts, or favors. Extortion is a form of blackmail.

graft: The use of government knowledge for personal gain.

influence peddling: Using influence with government officials to obtain favors for another person or group, generally for payment.

money laundering: Hiding the source of money that was obtained illegally, making it look like the funds came from a legitimate source.

nepotism: The act of people in power giving jobs to friends or relatives who are not qualified for that job.

tax evasion: Not paying the taxes that are owed to the government. This may involve not paying taxes at all or paying less than is owed.

interest group. One of the most famous scandals in American politics is known as Watergate. In the early 1970s, a group of men broke into the Democratic National Committee

DEMOCRACY IN DANGER

"Corruption is an insidious plague that ... undermines democracy and the rule of law, leads to violations of human rights, distorts markets, erodes the quality of life and allows organized crime, terrorism and other threats to human security to flourish."
—Kofi Annan, former United Nations (UN) secretary general

Quoted in Barbara Crossette, "Corruption's Threat to Democracy," *The Atlantic*, April 12, 2004. www.theatlantic.com/foreign/unwire/crossette2004-04-12.htm.

(DNC) headquarters, which was in a building complex called the Watergate. An investigation revealed that they were connected to then-president Richard Nixon. Further investigations uncovered that Nixon and his aides worked secretly to spy on and discredit his political enemies—not for monetary gain, but to hold on to political power. In Watergate, as in most corruption cases, all the activity took place in secret, because nobody involved wanted the public to know that their government was acting questionably. After the news of the scandal broke, the U.S. Senate Select Committee on Presidential Campaign Activities— often known as the Senate Watergate Committee— investigated Nixon and his officials. The committee approved three articles of impeachment (charges against a president to remove them from office) against Nixon. Before the scheduled impeachment vote on August 19, Nixon resigned on August 9, 1974. Watergate is so well-known even today that many scandalous events have "–gate" tacked on to the end of their name, such as Gamergate (a cyber mob that harassed any women who spoke out about sexism in the gaming industry), Deflategate (a National Football League scandal surrounding accusations that the New England Patriots under-inflated their footballs, making them easier for receivers and quarterbacks to handle), and Celebgate (the leak of private photos of celebrities, mostly women, on the internet in 2014).

No matter what the person's motivation, political corruption—the purpose of which is to serve private interests—is often viewed as the opposite of good governance. "Governance" is a term used to refer to the system and institutions created by a government to provide for the common good of its citizens. As an article in the *Connecticut Economy Quarterly* magazine stated, "Public officials are supposed to be trustees of the [commonwealth], not political buccaneers seeking their own private gain."[2]

The Most Corrupt in the World

Transparency International (TI) is a group that tracks corruption around the world. The group publishes an index that ranks countries according to their level of corruption, demonstrated through such realities as untrustworthy and badly functioning governments, judicial systems, and law enforcement. Each country is given a score out of 100; the closer to 0 the score is, the more corrupt the country is. The following table shows the most corrupt countries in the world as of 2018, according to TI's ranking system.

Country	Region and Score
1. Somalia	Sub-Saharan Africa (9)
2. South Sudan	Sub-Saharan Africa (12)
3. Syria	Middle East and North Africa (14)
4. Afghanistan	Asia Pacific (15)
5. Yemen	Middle East and North Africa (16)
6. Sudan	Middle East and North Africa (16)
7. Libya	Middle East and North Africa (17)
8. North Korea	Asia Pacific (17)
9. Guinea-Bissau	Sub-Saharan Africa (17)
10. Equatorial Guinea	Sub-Saharan Africa (17)

Fighting Corruption with Democracy

While democracy seems like it could be a safeguard against corruption, experts say that all types of governments are susceptible to it; governments are led by people, and the desire to satisfy one's own interests over the public interest is an all-too-human phenomenon. Despite this fact, many people argue that establishing democracies in developing countries can help reduce corruption.

Nondemocratic and more authoritarian nations typically have fewer checks and balances on official actions and much more secrecy surrounding government processes. Certainly, it is true that democracies tend to be more open, with a greater number of restrictions on behaviors that could be considered corrupt. However, democratic countries are hardly exempt from political corruption; the long string of political scandals in the United States is proof of this fact.

Even so, Yale political scientist and corruption scholar Susan Rose-Ackerman argues that the stronger the democracy, the lower the likelihood of corruption. For example, if a democracy has strong checks and balances and a clear separation of powers in place, such as the three branches of government in the United States, the risk of one entity having too much power is reduced. Theoretically, it makes it more difficult for individuals or groups wishing to influence government through corruption to succeed because the other branches of government can step in and take action against it.

Transparency, or the degree of openness and accountability, built into the democratic system is also important, experts say. If the public has access to information that can reveal possibly

Transparency in government must be a priority for all elected officials.

corrupt influences on government, whether through auditing and record-keeping systems or through a free and open press, citizens and voters can act as yet another check on government corruption.

A SYMPTOM IN THE SYSTEM

"[Corruption] is a symptom that the political system is operating with little concern for the broader public interest."
–Susan Rose-Ackerman, Yale political scientist

Susan Rose-Ackerman, *Corruption and Government: Causes, Consequences, and Reform.* New York, NY: Cambridge University Press, 1999, p. 226.

Straightforward Examples of Corruption

The most easily recognized types of political corruption are straightforward actions such as bribery, graft, and extortion. Other common forms of corruption include nepotism, fraud, embezzlement, and influence peddling.

In the United States, all of these forms of corruption are illegal. Laws have been passed that work to prevent and root out corruption in government. For example, under U.S. laws, any gift to the president of the United States worth more than $200 is considered a gift to the office of the presidency and not to the individual holding the office. If an outgoing president wants to keep the gift, he or she must pay for it. Of course, even in the presence of laws, criminal penalties, and law enforcement, some individuals still behave inappropriately. During Trump's presidential campaign, he pledged to "drain the swamp" when he took office, a metaphor for getting rid of corrupt officials. According to *Slate* magazine, this is a phrase that has been used in American politics since the early 1900s, proving that corruption has a long history in the United States, despite the checks, balances, and laws that have been passed to deal with it.

In some less developed or more autocratic countries, however, laws against corrupt behavior may not even exist. If they do, they may be weak or fail to be enforced, and blatant, or obvious, corruption such as bribery, graft, and nepotism are built into the political system and present at the highest levels of government. In fact, many heads of state throughout history have run organized systems of corruption to build their own wealth at the expense of the health and well-being of their people. Rulers such as Saddam Hussein in Iraq, Mohamed Suharto in Indonesia, and Nicolás Maduro in Venezuela are prime examples of this.

Mohamed Suharto was named one of the most corrupt political leaders of the 20th century.

Suharto, who ruled Indonesia from 1967 to 1998, was named by Transparency International (TI) as the most corrupt world leader of the past 20 years in 2004. He and his family reportedly stole up to $35 billion (U.S. equivalent) from Indonesia's government while he was in office. Under Suharto, the entire Indonesian economy was based on bribes to Suharto and his family. The system of corruption involved practices such as giving control of state-owned monopolies to family members and friends and requiring private companies to award stakes in the company to Suharto family members as a condition of doing business in Indonesia. In addition, under Suharto, all businesses and wealthy individuals were expected to "make donations," or give financial kickbacks, to a variety of corrupt "charitable" foundations that functioned as Suharto's personal banks. Corruption in Indonesia during this period was truly systemic.

More Subversive Forms of Political Corruption

While outright bribery and nepotism are the major concerns in autocratic or developing countries, less direct forms of political corruption are more common in developed democracies. As Rose-Ackerman explained, "In democracies corruption scandals are frequently associated with the financing of political campaigns."[3]

Because government officials in democracies must be elected to their positions, they may be accused of campaign finance corruption when they accept large financial contributions from individuals, companies, unions, or interest groups to fund or support their campaigns. Critics may claim that politicians are in the pocket of their funding sources and acting in favor of private interests to secure their election—something that is known as "vote buying"—although proof of these accusations has rarely been found. However, campaign finance reform has been a growing topic in modern American politics.

In the last few years, for instance, many people have been looking closely at the amount of money politicans take from the National Rifle Association (NRA). The number of shootings in public places, especially schools, has been increasing in the United States, and many have called for stricter gun control laws. Some politicians agree, but others have stated that restrictions would not have any effect on the number of shootings. In many cases, these politicians have received large campaign donations from the NRA over a number of years. For example, Florida Senator Marco Rubio has received more than $3 million from the NRA over the course of his career, according to the *Los Angeles Times*. In the wake of the February 2018 Marjory Stoneman Douglas High School shooting in Parkland, Florida, Rubio made statements that indicated he was unsure whether stricter laws would have prevented the tragedy from happening, despite data from other developed countries around the world showing that the amount of shootings decreased in those countries after laws that made it harder to get guns were passed. The NRA's donations have affected other policy decisions as well. For instance, in 2015, 54 senators voted against a bill that would forbid people on the government's terrorist watch list from purchasing a gun. These senators had collectively received $37 million from the NRA.

As the public begins to understand the extent of the NRA's involvement in politics, people have begun to protest. After the Parkland shooting, many people called for their elected representatives to turn down NRA donations, but whether they will do so remains to be seen, as the lure of campaign money can be strong. As the costs of running a campaign for elected office have steadily increased to levels that make it unaffordable for all but the richest people, candidates are pressured to raise huge amounts of money if they want to have any hope of being successful. Numerous reforms have been passed, but some campaigns have found new ways to get around each new legal requirement, allowing large amounts of private money to continue to pour into congressional and presidential elections. In fact, campaign finance is sometimes described by commentators as "legal corruption" because contributions are technically legal under existing campaign finance laws.

MONEY IS NOT THE ONLY FACTOR

"Money is a major factor in politics ... but so are parties and constituents and issues and interest groups and regional alliances and ideological factions and gender and ethnicity, and a host of factors."
—Gerald C. Lubenow, director of the Citizen's Research Foundation, a campaign finance research institute at the University of California, Berkeley

Gerald C. Lubenow, ed., *A User's Guide to Campaign Finance Reform.* New York, NY: Rowman & Littlefield, 2001, p. vii.

Lobbying and Corruption

Other forms of corruption that tend to arise in developed democracies involve high-paid lobbyists. Hired by corporations and interest groups, lobbyists are people who work to convince elected officials to support legislation or policies that might be beneficial or oppose policies that might be harmful to their specific, private interests. Lobbyists also work behind the scenes to coordinate and direct

Money is the most common reason people commit acts of corruption.

campaign contributions to elected officials. In fact, a lobbyist's job is to work tirelessly to keep the elected official informed of the interests of the lobbyist's employers, who are often major campaign funding sources.

Hiring and paying lobbyists is not an illegal act, but many countries try to regulate them to contain their influence on government. In the United States, for example, the Lobbying Disclosure Act of 1995, which was amended in 2007, requires lobbyists to register with the government and obey certain disclosure requirements. One rule prohibits lobbyists from bribing legislators with money or gifts.

In 2016, there were close to 10,000 lobbyists—most of them representing corporations or special interest groups—who were registered to lobby the nation's 535 members of Congress and other government officials. Many of the lobbying companies that employ lobbyists have offices on K Street in Washington, D.C., an area known as the center for national-level lobbying activities.

In rare cases, such as the Abramoff scandal, law enforcement is able to prove a case of direct bribery between lobbyists and government officials, where gifts, vacations, or financial rewards are unlawfully given by lobbyists to members of Congress to influence votes. For the most part, however, the influence of lobbyists and their money is implied rather than explicit. The elected official knows they are expected to favor the interests that funded their campaign. Although technically legal, many experts believe these forces have a powerful negative influence on the way laws and policies are made and enforced by the government.

Corruption may also arise with what is called the "revolving door" phenomenon. This is a common practice in the United States in which legislators, legislative staffers, and other government officials leave public office to take jobs as lobbyists for industry or special interest groups. They use their inside knowledge and professional contacts to influence legislation or government decisions to favor their new employers. According to a 2012 article published by the nonprofit research group Center for Public Integrity, at least 378 former House of Representative staffers became lobbyists at the end of 2009. About 80 percent of the former staffers worked for corporations, large industries, or lobbying firms. As journalist Elizabeth Drew explained in her 1999 book *The Corruption of American Politics,*

> *The main sources of this pool of access-sharks [are] the "money committees," such as the House and Senate Commerce Committees, which handle such issues as banking and telecommunications. Sometimes the former aides so draw on their expertise and are so drawn into the legislative considerations that they in effect still act as staff members, writing legislation, except for a lot more money.[4]*

Corporations and special interest groups often pay their lobbyists a lot of money, and this financial temptation is difficult to turn down. Once again, money helps people ignore any moral or ethical doubts, effectively enabling companies and groups to buy political influence.

Critics also often draw connections between the role of money in political campaigns and corporate fraud that can cause major financial losses for average citizens. Again, direct evidence of collusion between government officials and CEOs or other corporate officials is rare. In many cases, pro-corporate government policies or a lack of effective government oversight plays a significant part in creating the conditions for corporate fraud. These conditions are the natural result of close relationships between large industries and high-level politicians who depend on campaign contributions. Reformers argue that large corporations have a type and level of political influence that average citizens simply cannot match, and this influence sometimes results in corporate activities that bring great harm to taxpayers and the general public.

Lobbyists are shown here lined up outside a senator's office.

Undermining the Principles of Democracy

Many experts on political corruption argue that corruption in democratic governments undermines the central pillars of democracy. By producing legislators and officials who answer to special interests instead of citizens, corruption destroys the basic democratic principle that a government must be representative of the people and work for the public good. In turn, corrupt officials run the government and make policies that may unfairly allocate government services and benefits.

Some people have argued that the United States should no longer be considered a democracy because in many instances, politicians and companies do not listen to the will of the people. For example, when the House of Representatives passed a new health care bill in 2017, 55 percent of Americans disapproved of the bill and did not want it to pass, according to a survey conducted by National Public Radio (NPR). Many people called their representatives to ask them to vote against the bill, but it passed anyway before failing to pass in the Senate. In another example, residents of the town of Oxford, Massachusetts, were angry with their local water supply company because they believed it overcharged them and provided poor customer service. It was the only water company in town, so they could not switch to a different one; instead, they held a vote in 2014 to try to buy out the company so the citizens would be the ones who controlled their own water supply. In 2018, *The Atlantic* described what happened:

> *On the day of the crucial vote, the high-school auditorium swelled to capacity. Locals who had toiled on the issue for years noticed many newcomers—residents who hadn't showed up to previous town meetings about the buyout. When the vote was called, the measure failed—the company, called Aquarion, would remain the town's water supplier. Supporters of the buyout mounted a last-ditch effort to take a second vote, but before it could be organized, a lobbyist for Aquarion pulled a fire alarm. The building had to be evacuated, and the meeting adjourned. Aquarion retains control of Oxford's water system to this day.*[5]

Many people believed the voting process was unfair, although Aquarion denied accusations that it had asked its lobbyist to pull the alarm to prevent a second vote from taking place. *The Atlantic* noted that this is just one example of the fact that

> *across a range of issues, public policy does not reflect the preferences of the majority of Americans. If it did, the country would look radically different: Marijuana would be legal and campaign contributions more tightly regulated; paid parental leave would be the law of the land and public colleges free; the minimum wage would be higher and gun control much stricter; abortions would be more accessible in the early stages of pregnancy and illegal in the third trimester.*[6]

Meanwhile, a corrupt justice system erodes another important pillar of democracy—the rule of law, the idea that objective rules govern all citizens and apply equally to all citizens in the name of justice. A system that is corrupt and does not act in the public interest can ultimately become illegitimate in the eyes of its citizens, destroying the public's trust in their government.

Critics claim that corruption has become so widespread in the United States that its democratic system now favors those with the most money. Reformers in the United States argue that fundamental reform of campaign financing, lobby restrictions, and similar remedies are necessary to protect the very essence of American democracy.

International aid organizations and donors such as the United Nations (UN) and the World Bank also see corruption as a threat to democracy in the developing world. They have begun programs to work with developing nations to help reduce corruption. By strengthening citizen participation in government, providing for freedom of speech and expression, and implementing reforms that require government leaders to report their income, assets, campaign contributions, and other essential financial information, reformers believe they can help improve good governance and thereby reduce corruption around the globe.

Hindering Economic Development

In the past, some critics argued that bribes could help a country's economic development by getting around regulations that delayed necessary projects. However, it has become clear as

Unhealthy Corruption

A 2006 report on global health by TI concluded that corruption has a dramatic effect on public health around the world. The report found that in both developed and less developed nations, significant amounts of public funds that should be spent on health projects are lost to fraud and corruption. In Cambodia, for example, the organization found that between 5 and 10 percent of the health budget disappears before it is even transferred from the Ministry of Finance to the Ministry of Health. In some countries, patients must bribe doctors and health care workers before they can get adequate health care. Even in the United States, the authors of the study said, government-run health insurance programs such as Medicare and Medicaid lose 5 to 10 percent of their budget due to overpayment of health claims. Also, the report argued that some U.S. doctors are corrupted by drug companies that spend billions of dollars each year on free meals and other gifts to convince doctors to prescribe their products. As the organization stated, "Corruption in the health sector can mean the difference between life and death."[1] TI believes part of the solution to this problem is for governments to be more transparent with their financial information so it can be tracked more easily.

1. "Health," Transparency International, accessed on January 31, 2018. www.transparency.org/topic/detail/health.

time goes on that corruption—not regulation—is the thing that hinders economic development. When bribes become routine, the cost of doing business increases and competition decreases. Because only larger companies can afford to pay large bribes, corruption harms smaller businesses. These anticompetitive effects, in turn, often lower the quality of the products and services the companies provide. As with Aquarion, when a company knows it is the only option people have, it is likely to increase prices and care less about customer service. The people of Oxford wanted running water, so they kept giving Aquarion their business, even though they did not want to.

Economic consequences also occur when widespread corruption discourages potential foreign or domestic investors from providing financial support, drying up capital that might otherwise be available to help people start businesses or develop local resources. When government officials are pushed to make bad decisions about how to spend government funds, public resources are drawn away from social programs such as education, health, and infrastructure (building and maintaining structures such as roads, bridges, airports, and utilities). This diversion of funds often contributes to increased poverty in highly corrupt countries. As Columbia Business School economics professor Shang-Jin Wei concluded, "Evidence has clearly showed that domestic investment, foreign investment, and economic growth are lower in more corrupt countries."[7] Most experts today agree with Wei's conclusions.

A WORSENING PROBLEM

"The truth is, we have a system that thrives on corruption, and it's getting worse all the time."
–Bruce Berlin, author of *Breaking Big Money's Grip on America: Working Together to Revive Our Democracy*

Bruce Berlin, "America's Political System Thrives on Corruption," *Huffington Post*, March 24, 2017. www.huffingtonpost.com/entry/americas-political-system-thrives-on-corruption_us_58d55629e4b0f633072b371f.

Finding Solutions to the Problem

Many techniques have been used to combat political corruption, but determining the appropriate measure often depends on the conditions of corruption that exist in each country. Nevertheless, experts tend to agree on several key points that appear to create positive change. For less developed nations, experts say it is critical to create government transparency. It is essential to have a system of freedom of information, mandatory government reporting, open meetings (meetings anyone is allowed to attend), and other citizen participation laws designed to provide information to the public about the actions and decisions of government. It is also important for nations to pass laws designed to prevent corruption, such as anti-bribery and conflict-of-interest laws, codes of ethics, and laws that protect people who report corruption from being hurt or otherwise punished by the people they report. In addition, civil service reformers can reduce the temptation to take bribes by ensuring that government employees are reasonably paid and chosen based on how good they are at their job rather than through nepotism. None of these measures can be effective, however, without skilled law enforcement and an independent judiciary to uphold anti-corruption laws.

For more developed countries such as the United States, which already have these types of basic anti-corruption and transparency laws in place, the solution is different. In situations where the increasing role of money in elections and lobbying is present, reformers suggest a variety of solutions, such as campaign finance restrictions. These include strategies for reducing the influence of money in elections, such as offering public financing and free TV airtime to candidates. Experts recommend fighting the revolving door syndrome through restrictions on the places government employees can work once they leave government service.

However, not everyone agrees that corruption is always destructive or that reform is necessary. Some U.S. analysts, for example, argue that the right to spend money on politics is a form of free speech that is protected by the U.S. Constitution and that there is no concrete proof that money buys influence. They believe that money focuses candidates on issues that matter most to those who are willing to give money. Critics of this view say this means only the people with the most money will be able to have their concerns addressed—a system that benefits the rich and hurts the poor. In a democracy, they point out, decisions should be made based on a fair vote, not on the amount of money someone has.

CHAPTER 2

A Culture of Corruption

Since the founding of the United States, money and the corruption it can bring have plagued American democracy. Throughout U.S. history, private money has financed political elections; in the nation's early history, wealthy individuals used their financial power to influence elections and buy votes and favors. Over time, anti-corruption laws were passed in an attempt to stop this practice. The 20th century saw a series of important reforms; for instance, the notorious Watergate scandal brought about major campaign finance reforms. However, a 1976 U.S. Supreme Court decision cut back many of these reforms. The floodgates to corruption reopened, and huge amounts of money flowed into the U.S. political system once again.

The Way It Was

During America's early history, the notion of public service was quite different from what it is today. Bribes, favoritism, and other forms of what is now called corruption were common and accepted. Colonial governors sent from Great Britain increased their wealth through illegal dealings. Merchants made huge profits off the American Revolution by charging outrageous prices for goods needed by soldiers. Indeed, corruption was built into the foundation of the young country.

As the country began industrializing and expanding west, it created an opening for people to exploit opportunity. Powerful businessmen and ruthless investors routinely used bribes to buy political influence and manipulate government policies in ways that created great fortune for themselves and their associates. In fact, even President Abraham Lincoln tolerated widespread graft from his first war secretary, Simon Cameron, who supervised countless numbers of transportation and weapons contracts that drained the national treasury during the American Civil War.

In this political cartoon, Jay Gould is shown trying to corner the gold market, represented by the caged bulls and bears. Grant is in the background with a bag of gold, representing his role in the scandal.

Another example of widespread political corruption occurred during Ulysses S. Grant's presidential administration. Grant was a top Union Army general during the Civil War and became a national hero. He was later elected president. As the country returned to peacetime, the same group of crooked businessmen who profited off the war began to do business with the federal government, creating a massive rewards system that benefited a greedy few.

One of the most famous scandals during Grant's term was the Black Friday gold conspiracy, a scheme launched by war profiteers Jim Fisk and Jay Gould. The two tried to corner the nation's gold market by buying up gold and inflating the price so they could sell it at an enormous profit. When Grant realized how bad this would be for the economy, he ordered the government to sell $5 million in gold. This caused the gold market to crash, bringing financial ruin to many Wall Street investors in 1869.

State and local politics were plagued by widespread corruption during this period as well. As the political magazine the *Nation* complained in 1868, "There is hardly a legislature in the country that is not suspected of corruption; there is hardly a court over which the same suspicion does not hang."[8] This was the era of the notorious William M. "Boss" Tweed, a New York politician who was elected to the House of Representatives in 1852, the New York City Board of Advisors in 1856, and the New York State Senate in 1868.

Tweed ran Tammany Hall, a Democratic Party political machine that was at the heart of New York political thievery for many decades. Tweed organized the city's new immigrant groups and bought votes to help candidates get elected. In exchange for his influence, politicians then looked the other way while Tweed and his partners embezzled as much as $200 million from the New York City government.

Tweed was convicted of forgery and larceny (theft) in 1873, but he left a legacy of political patronage and corruption that plagued New York City politics for many more years. By the time the country celebrated its 100th birthday in 1876, bribery, graft, and political patronage were still very real problems in American democracy.

Tammany Hall, which was run by Boss Tweed, was a group that effectively controlled the New York Democratic Party during the 19th century.

Progressivism to the Rescue

The public's view of America's long tradition of corruption soon turned to disgust, and there was a push for reform. Industrialization and the massive wave of corruption after the Civil War created a push for social reforms led by people who called themselves Progressives. The Progressives' first victory was convincing Congress to pass the Pendleton Civil Service Act of 1883—legislation that created the nation's first merit-based civil service system. Before this legislation passed, government jobs were won only through a system of patronage, in which jobs were given to friends, relatives, or people who offered bribes. In the 1880s, for example, it was not uncommon for newspapers to carry ads such as the following: "WANTED—A GOVERNMENT CLERKSHIP at a salary of not less than $1,000 per annum. Will give $100 to any one securing me such a position."[9] The Pendleton Civil Service Act established a system of civil service exams, which meant that federal government jobs would now be filled based on specific qualifications. It also prohibited federal workers from making contributions to political campaigns to get or keep their jobs. This system still functions today; to get jobs such as library clerk, police chief, prison security guard, and certain medical positions, people must have the appropriate degree and experience, just as with any other job. However, in addition, they must also get a certain score on an exam that tests their knowledge. The score may vary depending on the type and location of the job. There is often a small application fee—generally less than $40—that is meant to be used by the government to pay for filing and scoring the exams.

However, by cutting off the stream of payments from federal workers and job seekers, the Pendleton Civil Service Act promoted an increase of corporate contributions to political campaigns. In the 1896 presidential race, for example, wealthy Cleveland, Ohio, industrialist Marcus Alonzo Hanna raised a shockingly large amount—$4 million, which would be more than $111 million in 2018—for Republican candidate William McKinley. This money is credited with helping McKinley win the presidency; McKinley spent more than 10 times the amount spent by his opponent, Democrat William Jennings Bryan. By the end of the 19th century, the amount of corporate money in elections had reached alarming levels.

The 1904 presidential election, however, marked a turning point for American campaign financing. President Theodore Roosevelt was accused by Democratic opponent Alton B. Parker of accepting large corporate contributions during his campaign; in response, Roosevelt proposed a ban on all corporate contributions. Progressive activists took up Roosevelt's call and pushed for reform; Congress finally responded in 1907 with the passage of the Tillman Act, a law that prohibited corporations and national banks from contributing to federal campaigns. The Tillman Act was the first federal law to address campaign financing.

The passage of the Tillman Act was the momentum the Progressives needed. They continued to press for more reforms and next focused on making information about campaign donations available to the public. They argued that publicizing the source of campaign donations would allow citizens to evaluate whether legislators were beholden to contributors, meaning that they might feel required to repay contributors with political favors. This pressure resulted in the 1910 Publicity Act, which required federal congressional candidates to reveal all spending and contributions at the end of election campaigns. The act, which was amended in 1911, also established the first spending limits for federal campaigns: $5,000 for House campaigns and $10,000 for Senate contests. The spending limits, however, were quickly challenged, and in 1921, the Supreme Court decision in *Newberry v. United States* struck down the spending limits, ruling that Congress had no authority to regulate primary elections.

Political Scandals on Public Lands

Despite these reforms, corruption continued to be a problem at the highest levels of government. The election of President Warren G. Harding in 1920 led to the Teapot Dome political scandal, which involved the leasing, or renting, of oil fields located on public lands.

Harding's friend and secretary of the interior, Albert B. Fall, awarded a series of long-term lease contracts worth about $200 million to two large U.S. oil companies in exchange for loans and gifts totaling more than $400,000. When Fall's sudden wealth attracted attention, Harding defended him, but Fall was eventually convicted of bribery in 1929 and sentenced to one

Shown here are the president and vice president of Sinclair Oil (second and third from right, respectively), testifying about their role in the Teapot Dome Scandal.

year in prison. Fall, however, was only one of many corrupt Harding appointees. As author Nathan Miller explained,

> [Harding's] interior secretary became the first cabinet member to go to jail; his attorney general only narrowly escaped a similar fate; and his secretary of the navy was forced to resign as a result of a mixture of stupidity and criminal negligence. Fraud in the Veterans Bureau, graft in the Office of the Alien Property Custodian, and conspiracy in the Justice Department were all part of Harding's legacy.[10]

Reformers rallied against the corruption in Harding's administration, and reform efforts gained more support, leading to the passage of yet another piece of reform legislation—the Federal Corrupt Practices Act of 1925, which replaced and repealed parts of the Publicity Act. This legislation reinstated campaign spending limits for candidates running in congressional races, with Senate campaigns capped at $25,000 and House campaigns limited to $5,000. However, the new legislation did not include primary elections because of the Newberry decision. The 1925 act also required national political parties to file contributions and expenditures reports and tightened previous disclosure rules by requiring quarterly reports, even in non-election years.

Two other pieces of reform legislation passed during this era. One was the Hatch Act of 1939, which was later amended in 1940. This law prohibited various forms of political activity by federal workers. Federal employees were banned from soliciting, or asking for, campaign contributions, which was then a common source of income for state and local political parties. The law also established limits for federal campaign contributions. Individual contributions were limited to $5,000 per year, and political parties could not collect more than $3 million in contributions. The final reform during this time was the 1943 Smith-Connally

MONEY IS THE GOAL

"The culture of money dominates Washington as never before; money now rivals or even exceeds power as the preeminent goal."
—Elizabeth Drew, political journalist and author

Elizabeth Drew, *The Corruption of American Politics: What Went Wrong and Why*. New York, NY: Overlook, 1999, p. 64.

Anti-Strike Act, also called the War Labor Disputes Act, which included a provision that prohibited labor unions from making political contributions to federal candidates.

"Pervasive Evasion and Non-Enforcement"

Despite reformers' best efforts, early anti-corruption reforms failed to accomplish their stated aims. Corporations quickly figured out ways to get around laws such as the Tillman Act; for example, businesses simply awarded bonuses to their employees with the understanding that the employees would give the money to candidates endorsed by the company. Many laws, such as the Publicity Act, failed to build in enforcement measures. Spending limits were too easy to ignore. As the late political scientist Frank Sorauf put it, "The reality was one of pervasive evasion and non-enforcement."[11]

Large amounts of corporate money continued to pour into American politics throughout the 1950s, 1960s, and 1970s. Election campaigns became increasingly expensive as radio and television advertising became more common than traditional forms such as newspaper ads and billboards. Television, in particular, revolutionized politics and dramatically affected the costs of political campaigns. According to Sorauf, "Television costs in the general election of 1956 had been $6.6 million, but by 1968 they had shot up to $27.1 million."[12]

This period, however, was not defined by the large-scale bribery scandals of the past. Instead, corruption in American politics did not go away; it just became more subtle and sophisticated than the corruption of years past. Corporations also began to take a bigger role in corrupt practices. During Harry S. Truman's administration from 1945 to 1953, several officials appointed by the president became involved in small-time bribery incidents, bringing great embarrassment to Truman. One of these officials was General Harry Vaughan, who used his influence with the White House to help certain companies gain preferential treatment from government agencies. In return, Vaughan and other Truman officials received several deep freezers, which were hard to find in the postwar period. The freezers became a symbol of corruption for the Truman administration.

General Harry Vaughan (far left) embarrassed President Harry Truman (second from left) by becoming involved in corruption.

The fallout of the Truman scandals helped Dwight D. Eisenhower win the presidency in 1952, but during the campaign, the news broke that his running mate, Richard Nixon, had received payments from millionaires to fund his political activities. Nixon managed to survive by making an emotional speech on nationwide television—a speech popularly known as "Checkers" because he claimed the only gift he would keep was a dog named Checkers. Nevertheless, the Eisenhower administration, as well as the following administrations of John F. Kennedy and Lyndon B. Johnson, had to deal with scandals involving bribery and corruption.

Costs of presidential campaigns continued to skyrocket, and by the 1970s, concerns over campaign costs once again created a climate for reform. In 1971, Congress responded to these concerns with two major reform bills. The Revenue Act authorized a public financing plan that allowed taxpayers to donate $1 of their taxes to a public campaign fund for presidential and vice presidential campaigns. If they wanted to participate, taxpayers could check a box on their tax return form. This law was passed, but the option did not appear on tax forms until

REINFORCING THE MESSAGE

"People don't like ... [negative ads], but they work ... Repetition is what it takes to make the message stick, and positive ads need a lot more repetition than negative ones."
—Steve McMahon, founder of McMahon, Squier and Associates, a media consulting firm in the Washington, D.C., area

Quoted in Mark Green, *Selling Out: How Big Corporate Money Buys Elections, Rams Through Legislation, and Betrays Our Democracy.* New York, NY: Regan Books, 2002, p. 116.

several years later. The second piece of legislation was the 1971 Federal Election Campaign Act (FECA), a law that replaced earlier reporting and disclosure requirements with a strengthened plan that required candidates and parties to disclose more detailed information. FECA also applied to political parties and political action committees (PACs), groups formed to raise money for political candidates. The act also attempted to limit rising campaign costs by limiting the amount candidates could contribute to their own campaigns. This applied to both congressional and presidential candidates. Spending on media advertising—including television, radio, magazines, newspapers, and billboards—was similarly limited.

MONEY TALKS

"It is difficult to represent the little fellow when the big fellow pays the tab."
–Robert Reich, secretary of labor during the administration of Bill Clinton

Quoted in Mark Green, *Selling Out: How Big Corporate Money Buys Elections, Rams Through Legislation, and Betrays Our Democracy.* New York, NY: Regan, 2002, p. 116.

In the Wake of Watergate

For all the scandals in American politics, none quite matched the scope of Nixon's Watergate scandal. Several serious reforms followed Watergate, which is still one of the biggest political scandals ever to hit the United States.

The scandal began in 1972 when operatives of then-president Richard Nixon, a Republican, burglarized and bugged (hid recording devices in) the offices of the Democratic National Committee (DNC) in the Watergate building in Washington, D.C., to gain political advantage. The idea was for Nixon's team to learn what the Democrats were planning to do in the upcoming presidential campaign so Nixon could have a better chance of getting reelected. An investigation revealed that Nixon's reelection committee had also created a secret—and illegal—campaign fund containing hundreds of thousands of dollars of undisclosed donations. The funds were used to pay off the

The Senate Watergate Committee delivered its final report on the Senate hearings in 1974.

Watergate burglars so they would remain silent during their criminal trials. Later investigations revealed that Nixon also relied on huge corporate contributions for his presidential campaigns and that people who had donated large amounts of money were rewarded with political positions by the Nixon administration. Nixon was forced to resign in 1974, and over the next several years, Congress focused on passing a series of laws known as the Watergate reforms.

The most significant reform of this period was a 1974 amendment to FECA that virtually rewrote the original law. The amended law created the first program of public campaign funding for presidential elections. This program allowed U.S. presidential candidates to choose full public financing for general election campaigns and partial subsidies, or contributions, for primary campaigns in exchange for limiting private donations. The law aimed to reduce the pressures of raising campaign money and encourage candidates to ask for small donations from average citizens. The program operated through a voluntary contribution on federal income tax forms, the same idea contained in the Revenue Act of 1971 (which had been passed but not yet implemented). The FECA amendment effectively replaced the Revenue Act before it could be put in place. In 1994, this contribution was raised from $1 to $3.

The act also strengthened disclosure provisions and set new limits on campaign contributions and expenditures. Individual contribution limits were set at $1,000 per candidate, an additional $1,000 for candidate advertising, $5,000 for donations to PACs, and a combined amount of $25,000 for all contributions to all federal candidates, parties, or PACs. PACs were permitted to collect only relatively small donations of $5,000 each year from individuals and were limited to contributing $5,000 per candidate. Candidates themselves were limited to spending only $50,000 of their own money if they wanted to accept public financing. Additionally, the act established the Federal Election Commission (FEC), an independent agency tasked with enforcing the new rules.

Watergate also produced a series of other government reforms. The 1974 Freedom of Information Act, for example, allowed ordinary citizens to obtain copies of public documents and records. In theory, this increased accountability on the part of government officials. The 1976 Government in the Sunshine Act required federal government agencies to conduct open meetings, although there were certain exceptions. In 1978, Congress passed the Ethics in Government Act, which created a special prosecutor (later called independent counsel) position that could be used by Congress or the attorney general to investigate the conduct of people who held high positions in the government. Also in 1978, Congress enacted federal whistleblower legislation to prevent retaliation against people who expose government corruption.

Dealing a Blow to Reform

FECA and the Watergate reforms seemed to signal a shift in the tides of political corruption, with many laws now in place to combat it. However, the cause suffered a setback in 1976, when the U.S. Supreme Court dealt a deathblow to many of FECA's provisions. In the landmark case *Buckley v. Valeo*, the Supreme Court ruled parts of the act unconstitutional because they violated the First Amendment. For the first time, political campaign spending was entitled to constitutional free speech protections. Specifically, the ruling eliminated all of FECA's spending limits, as well as limits on contributions made by candidates themselves or made by citizens or PACs for so-called independent expenditures, such as advertising that was not connected with a candidate's campaign. The Court upheld the remaining parts of FECA, which include its disclosure requirements, the public financing program, and the individual, party, and PAC limits on direct campaign contributions.

Experts claim that the court decision unleashed a new wave of corporate money into elections; the decision allowed unlimited amounts to be spent on campaigns and created a climate in which wealthy candidates were more successful in running for office. Also, by introducing the concept of independent expenditures, *Buckley v. Valeo* encouraged a whole new trend of expensive television advertisements, called issue ads, paid for by PACs set up by corporations and other special interest groups. As long as the ads were independent—meaning that they did not coordinate directly with campaigns or use any of a list of words that the Supreme Court said would constitute express advocacy on behalf of or against a candidate (such as "vote for," "elect," or "defeat")—there was absolutely no limit to the amount of money that could be spent. In recent years, people have stretched the legal definition of an issue ad by simply avoiding the specific words mentioned by the Supreme Court, blurring the line between issue advocacy and express advocacy. For example, many people are familiar with ads that run during an election year that say things such as, "Candidate A supports policies that are bad for small businesses. Candidate B opposes those policies." As long as the ad does not specifically tell people to elect Candidate B, it is generally considered an issue ad even though it is clearly supporting a particular candidate. Advocacy ads are required to disclose where their funding came from; at the end of this type of ad, the announcer may something such as, "Paid for by the Committee to Elect Candidate B." Issue ads are not required to give this disclaimer, which means it is harder for people who hear or see the ad to know who is trying to influence their opinion. This is a loophole in the law that many candidates have taken advantage of since it was passed, allowing them to spend millions of dollars on campaign advertising, getting around the law that was intended to limit that spending.

Not surprisingly, the number of PACs skyrocketed after the Buckley decision, and issue ads became the new weapon of choice in political campaigns. For example, supporters of George H. W. Bush used negative ads during the 1992 presidential campaign to create a negative image of Democratic challenger Bill Clinton. In that race, a conservative lobbying group called the Christian Action Network used a negative issue ad to criticize Clinton's support for homosexual rights. The $2 million ad aired more than 250 times in 24 major cities across the country and featured

Clinton policy statements mixed with pictures of young men marching in a Gay Pride parade. The ad implied that homosexuality, which was less widely accepted than it is today, would ruin America. The FEC challenged the ad but lost in federal court because the words specifically banned by the Buckley case were not used. Since then, the use of issue ads has exploded.

The Impact of *Buckley v. Valeo*

Since it was issued in 1976, the U.S. Supreme Court's decision in *Buckley v. Valeo* has aroused frequent criticism. Many campaign finance reform experts believe that Buckley's ruling—that limits on campaign spending were an unconstitutional infringement on free speech—was badly reasoned. Constitutional law holds that limits on free speech are allowed only if they serve a compelling government interest.

The Court in 1976 found that the only compelling government interest would be prevention of corruption and that spending limits failed to serve this interest. Critics charge, however, that there are other compelling interests at stake, such as the need to maintain a fully representative democracy, in which elected officials represent public rather than private interests. The Court's failure to consider this larger issue, critics say, is the primary reason that the United States has been unable to control the problem of money in politics.

Despite this criticism, the Court has shown no signs that it intends to overturn or modify the *Buckley v. Valeo* ruling. As recently as 2014, the Supreme Court used the *Buckley v. Valeo* ruling in *McCutcheon v. Federal Election Commission* when it upheld that limiting campaign giving by individuals is unconstitutional.

Legal Loopholes

There was no shortage of loopholes found to circumvent, or get around, FECA's provisions. For example, using a technique called bundling, individuals or companies can collect

FOOTING THE BILL

"Money cannot be entirely eliminated from politics.
Elections must be financed and wealthy interests
concerned with legislative outcomes and government
policy may be willing to foot the bill."
—Susan Rose-Ackerman, Yale political scientist

Susan Rose-Ackerman, *Corruption and Government: Causes, Consequences, and Reform.* New York,
NY: Cambridge University Press, 1999, pp. 132–133.

contributions from family members, friends, or employees and
then deliver the combined donation to a particular candidate
with a clear understanding that it is all coming from one place.
This makes candidates as beholden as if that person or company
had directly made the large donation while still abiding by the
law that no more than $1,000 can come from any individual.

Soft money, which refers to funds not regulated by federal
laws, is a bit more complicated. Because state and local political parties complained that the FECA spending limits restricted
them from doing grassroots political activities such as voter
registration and get-out-the-vote drives, Congress passed new
amendments to FECA in 1979 that granted party organizations a limited exemption from spending limits. Under the new
law, as interpreted by the FEC, parties could collect and spend
unlimited amounts of money on these types of local political
activities. Hard money, in contrast, is money that is subject to
those regulations.

Soon, however, political parties used these exemptions to
fund issue ads as well, stretching the limits of FECA to new levels.
This dramatically expanded the role political parties played in
campaigns, allowing them to become the primary sponsor of
expensive issue ads. Eventually, all of these loopholes made the
anti-corruption reforms put in place after Watergate completely
useless. Although donations to candidates were still subject to
limits, unlimited amounts of soft money could be used to buy
ads and otherwise indirectly support specific candidates.

CHAPTER 3

The Role of Money

Loopholes, amendments, Supreme Court decisions, and weakness in laws mean that an incredible amount of money continues to pour in for political elections and lobbying activity. As long as they have the money, millionaires, corporations, unions, and special interest groups can finance the political interests that are important to them. For politicians, these donations come at a price. Although candidates benefit by receiving large amounts of campaign funds, they have to spend much of their time focused on raising those funds, and they may lose control of their campaign if they have to later answer to donors. Critics say money has created a deeply entrenched culture of corruption that has had disastrous results for ordinary Americans.

Pay to Win

Buckley v. Valeo and loopholes in campaign finance laws have led to an enormous increase in the money it takes to win elections. These days, hopeful politicians have to pay to campaign and win elections. As Democratic politician and author Mark Green explained, "While in 1976 it cost an average of $87,000 to win a House seat and $609,000 a U.S. Senate seat, those amounts grew by 2000 like beanstalks to $842,000 for the House and $7.2 million for the Senate—a tenfold leap."[13]

Reports from the 2016 Senate elections showed that winning Senate candidates spent an average of $10.4 million dollars, an increase of $1.8 million over the average in 2014. While not every candidate spent that amount of money, some were big spenders. For instance, Senator Pat Toomey of Pennsylvania spent a reported $27.8 million on his 2016 campaign, which was just a fraction of the total cost of the state's 2016 Senate race. Altogether, Pennsylvania spent $164 million, which was made up of both the candidates' campaign spending and outside spending.

Presidential campaigns, too, cost more each election. In the 2004 presidential election, for example, President George W. Bush and Senator John Kerry both rejected public funding during the primary phase, allowing them together to raise almost $1 billion in private financing; then, during the general election, they each received an additional $74.6 million in government funding. More than a decade later, costs rose to a record-breaking high. In 2016, presidential candidate Hillary Clinton spent more than $1 billion in the race to become president.

The major cost for campaigns is the increasingly expensive broadcast time for TV ads. Free airtime is not required, and even scheduled debates between the candidates are sometimes not broadcast by the various television networks. The candidate who does not win the fund-raising battle often loses the election. In fact, 94 percent of congressional races are won by the big spenders, regardless of the candidates' qualifications, skills, or voting records.

Experts say the quest for big money has changed the way the president and members of Congress run for office. Today, fund-raising is the paramount priority during campaigns. As Mark Green explained, "Thanks to today's high-cost races, candidates spend very little time running in the traditional sense of the word—mobilizing voters, communicating ideas, debating opponents, attending public meetings. Instead, candidates fund-raise for office."[14]

The push for fund-raising only continues once candidates are elected. In a 2016 interview, Florida congressman David Jolly said that when he was first elected, a party leader laid the reality of fund-raising on the table:

> We sat behind closed doors at one of the party headquarter back rooms in front of a white board where the equation was drawn out. You have six months until the election. Break that down to having to raise $2 million in the next six months. And your job, new member of Congress, is to raise $18,000 a day. Your first responsibility is to make sure you hit $18,000 a day.[15]

This issue was further discussed on the political entertainment show *Last Week Tonight with John Oliver*. Several politicians were quoted on the program as saying that they hated this part of their job, but they did it because it was a political necessity. Some politicians have used events such as their own birthday party or a Taylor Swift concert as an excuse to hold a fund-raiser, selling tickets to the events for hundreds or thousands of dollars.

Fund-raising efforts sometimes even interrupt the lawmakers' jobs. As Representative Carolyn McCarthy said,

The first week I was down here, we were having a committee hearing on education and my chief of staff at that time came in and said, "You have to leave." You know, and we went into the anteroom and I said, "Where do I have to go?" And she goes, "Well, you have to go make phone calls." And I looked at her and I went, "This is my first hearing and you're coming in and asking me to leave? How am I going to learn anything?"[16]

Legislators are expected to spend about four hours per day making phone calls to ask voters for money, although by federal law, they are not allowed to make these calls in their offices. For this reason, they must go to call centers set up in their party's headquarters. Even when they do not need funds for their own campaigns, they are expected to help raise money for the party so it can be distributed to those who need to spend more money on advocacy ads. Each member is expected to pay between $125,000 and $800,000, making fund-raising necessary for all but the richest members of Congress. Representative Steve Israel retired in 2016, saying it was because "I don't think I can spend another day in another call room making another call begging for money."[17] Throughout his 16 years in Congress, he said, he attended 1,600 fund-raising events for his reelection alone, and he noted that the

Large fund-raising events are key to helping candidates raise the money they need to get elected.

people who attended those fund-raising events made it clear that they expected him to vote the way they wanted him to in exchange for their donation.

Critics say this preoccupation with raising money negatively affects politicians' job performance. Both congressional representatives and presidents, for example, are spending less and less time on the people's business. Too often, critics say, there is a widespread reluctance by incumbents (people who are currently in office) to take on controversial issues or issues that are unpopular with major funding sources, for fear of losing career-sustaining campaign dollars. In light of legislators' pressing financial priorities, some commentators say it is no wonder that Congress has developed a reputation among voters for doing nothing.

If incumbents ever forget who is paying for their reelection, the army of corporate and special interest lobbyists will quickly remind them. As the representatives for their employers, these lobbyists set up all kinds of contributions that bring money or other benefits to members of Congress or their districts. These include not only direct campaign contributions from company employees and PACs, but also unlimited soft money donations that are used to host fund-raising dinners and events, charitable organizations favored by legislators, or special projects that might bring jobs or tourist dollars to a legislator's home state or district. The same system infects the executive branch.

On the *Last Week Tonight with John Oliver* segment, Senator Chris Murphy raised an important point about where legislators' money comes from. He said he targets people who can easily afford to give $1,000, which means the issues these donors want their representatives to address are much different than the issues people who live in poverty want to see changed.

All this money buys enormous access to Congress as well as to other government officials—close contact that ordinary citizens do not have. This access may buy officials' votes or sway decisions on key policies and pieces of legislation, but often, the more common outcome is much more subtle: influence. In Congress, this might take several different forms. A politician might vote to prevent bills or certain parts of bills from ever being reported outside of congressional committees, or they might quietly add a rider that benefits a private interest into larger bills that are sure to pass. A rider is a provision that has little or no connection to a bill; it is a way to get laws that have little support passed. For instance, a bill about education reform might include a rider that gives tax cuts to a corporation. Access might also convince government officials to block or change government regulations, influence regulatory decisions, help secure government contract awards, or achieve some other form of behind-the-scenes advocacy that benefits campaign donors.

Close examination of corruption in American politics makes one thing plain: The general public suffers most in all of this. Reformers say big money in politics unquestionably results in government policies that are geared toward the needs of corporate contributors rather than the needs of ordinary citizens. These effects are often very difficult to prove, and most of the time, they are hidden from the general public. Sometimes, however, information about this system leaks out, resulting in much-publicized scandals and causing the public to suspect all politicians of corruption. As Senator John McCain said, "We're all tainted ... [All members of Congress are] under suspicion as long as Washington is awash in special interest money."[18]

THE VIEW AT THE TOP

"If the only people you ever talk to are people with the wherewithal to contribute thousands of dollars to your campaign, that is bound to affect the way you see the world."
–James Carville, political consultant

James Carville and Paul Begala, "Not One Dime: A Radical Plan to Abramoff-Proof Politics," *Washington Monthly*, March 2006, p. 14.

Political Scandals in the Modern Era

Since the series of reforms that passed in the 1970s, the United States has seen its fair share of modern corruption scandals affecting virtually every recent presidential administration. Even reform-minded Jimmy Carter, the first elected president after

Watergate (Nixon's vice president Gerald Ford, who was sworn in after Nixon resigned, served from 1974 to 1977), suffered from minor scandals during his 1977 to 1981 term in office. His own brother, for example, accepted a $220,000 loan from the country of Libya to assist with oil sales to America, and the press accused him of selling his influence with the White House.

The administration of President Ronald Reagan in the 1980s, however, brought more serious political scandals. As Nathan Miller explained,

> While preaching against waste, fraud, and abuse of government power, he [Reagan] presided for eight years over an administration that combined the old-fashioned graft of the Grant and Harding eras with an undisguised grab for power ... Thievery and manipulation occurred on a grand scale and the amount of loot took a quantum leap compared to previous corruption.[19]

One of the many scandals that arose during Reagan's two terms in office was a major corruption investigation into the Department of Housing and Urban Development (HUD) and its secretary, Samuel R. Pierce Jr. Although HUD was supposed to help with housing for the poor, under Pierce's reign, HUD funds were used to build luxury country clubs, golf courses, and other projects favored by members of Congress or government officials. HUD officials were also found to have embezzled funds and directed projects to Reagan supporters without competitive bidding to keep things fair. Neither Pierce nor Reagan took steps to halt the widespread corruption at HUD.

Reagan's laissez-faire, or hands-off, attitude toward corruption helped it spread throughout his government. By the end of Reagan's presidency, as Miller explained, "as many as 225 of his appointees faced allegations [accusations] of ethical or criminal wrongdoing."[20] Presidents who followed

Samuel R. Pierce Jr. was at the center of a major scandal during the Reagan administration.

Reagan have also been criticized for activities that, at the very least, gave the appearance of corruption. Republican George H. W. Bush, for example, was frequently linked with international influence-peddling deals during his 1989 to 1993 presidential term. According to political analyst Kevin Phillips, a number of Bush's relatives made personal fortunes during his presidency, largely with the help of President Bush's network of wealthy fund-raisers and supporters. Additionally, Bush's son George W. Bush (who was later elected president) acquired shares in Harken Energy, a small company with no overseas oil-drilling experience that nevertheless, during his father's presidency, won a major oil-drilling contract from Bahrain, as well as direct access to President Bush and his foreign policy advisers.

In 1990, George W. Bush made a quick $848,000 profit by suddenly selling his Harken shares just before the company's stock prices dropped dramatically. The deal demonstrated aspects of insider trading, which is when people have secret knowledge of a company's profits, allowing them to make decisions about their investments that will make them a profit. Insider trading is illegal because it gives an unfair advantage to certain people, so George W. Bush was investigated by the Securities and Exchange Commission (SEC). The SEC, then headed by a former aide to President George H. W. Bush, Richard Breeden, issued no ruling against the president's son.

Several George H. W. Bush administration officials, too, were criticized for conflicts of interest that increased their personal wealth. One was treasury secretary James A. Baker, who approved policies that benefited U.S. banks while he held a large chunk of stock in one bank, resulting in a 40 percent personal profit.

The culture of corruption carried across party lines to the next U.S. president, Bill Clinton, a Democrat who was elected in 1992. Some of the most serious allegations against Clinton occurred when news leaked out that the People's Republic of China tried to make numerous large donations to the DNC and other Democratic causes just before Clinton's 1996 reelection campaign. Such donations by foreign citizens or governments to U.S. political candidates or campaigns are illegal under U.S. law. The largest donations, including a $460,000 cash donation to Clinton's legal defense fund and $220,000 to the DNC, were made by a Chinese

Corruption in Arms

In 1986, the Reagan administration became caught up in a political scandal known as Iran-Contra. This scandal involved the sale of military arms, or weapons, to Iran, a U.S. enemy, in order to free American hostages that were being held by the terrorist group Hezbollah. The profits from these arms sales were then secretly used to fund anti-Communist rebel groups, the Contras, who were fighting to overturn the South American government of Nicaragua.

The Iran-Contra operation was run by William Casey, the director of the Central Intelligence Agency (CIA), and Marine Lieutenant Colonel Oliver L. North, a staffer at the National Security Council (NSC). The scandal was problematic in two key ways: It defied Reagan's stated policy to never bargain with terrorists for hostages, and the aid given to the Contras was a direct violation of the Boland Amendment, a law that prohibited such activities. Just as in Watergate, high-level government officials broke the law to achieve political power and policy goals.

An investigation produced several criminal convictions, but Casey died before the investigation was completed. North's conviction for perjury, or lying in court, was overturned on technicalities. Six other Iran-Contra defendants were pardoned by George H. W. Bush when he became president.

Members of the Iran-Contra committee held a press conference to answer questions following the release of the committee's report.

American friend of Clinton's who was suspected of working for the Chinese. Clinton's attorney general Janet Reno refused to appoint an independent counsel to look into the possibility of widespread fund-raising abuses by the administration, sparking rumors of a cover-up. The Justice Department's own investigation, however, ended with 17 convictions for campaign finance irregularities, many of them against Clinton's personal friends.

The nation's next president, George W. Bush, has been repeatedly criticized for his questionable business dealings and easy acquisition of wealth during his father's presidential term, and almost a decade later, for corruption within his own administration. For instance, one scandal during the George W. Bush administration involved the awarding of multibillion-dollar Iraq War contracts to Halliburton, a company once headed by Vice President Dick Cheney, and other companies with close ties to the administration, without engaging in a competitive bidding process. As the war progressed, government investigators discovered that a company controlled by Halliburton had severely overcharged the U.S. government for supplies such as meals and fuel—an example of war profiteering straight out of the past.

Corruption and Hillary Clinton

When President Barack Obama took office in 2008, citizens hoped to leave the corruption of the past behind. However, the Obama administration did not avoid controversy altogether, and some top officials made headlines for questionable actions. One of the most discussed was the email scandal regarding Obama's secretary of state, Hillary Clinton. Clinton used a personal email address on a privately-owned server, rather than an email address and server owned by the government. This had been done in the past, but "Clinton's approach was particularly controversial because it's out of step with typical government practice now and gave Clinton a major measure of control over what remains private and what's public."[21] This, many people feared, would give her an opportunity to do unethical things without being caught. Government officials' emails are not supposed to be private for exactly that reason. She was also accused of having deleted many emails that people believed might have proven that she had done

Political Culture Encourages Corruption

The website Cracked interviewed several people who have worked in politics to learn about how the culture of politics influences corruption. According to a member of the 2012 Electoral College,

> There's a country-club cattiness about it. "He's been driving that same car for three years," even though when you're with constituents [voters you represent] you brag about having an old car. It's a status thing ... Who has the most money for the next campaign? Who has the biggest PAC? Who had Karl Rove come speak at their fundraiser?[1]

This obsession with appearances can encourage politicians to turn to corrupt practices to stay well-regarded in the eyes of their peers.

Additionally, much of the corruption that takes place in government is not legally considered bribery. According to Jack Abramoff, many politicians would feel uncomfortable taking a bribe if it were offered outright. He said,

> You need a quid pro quo for it to be statutory bribery [i.e.: I vote this way, you pay me] ... Instead, they bribe in a far more palatable [pleasant] and legal way ... They take Congress to ball games, dinner, golf, and concerts. They provide thousands of dollars in campaign contributions. The congressman, in turn, being grateful for all this bounty, lends an ear or hand to the lobbyist when needed.[2]

Many politicians get so used to these types of benefits, according to the Cracked interviewees, that they start to expect them and do not feel they are doing anything wrong by accepting them.

1. Quoted in Robert Evans, "6 Insane Details of Corrupt Politics that Movies Get Wrong," Cracked, October 7, 2014. www.cracked.com/personal-experiences-1472-6-ways-government-corruption-way-weirder-than-you-think.html.
2. Quoted in Evans, "6 Insane Details of Corrupt Politics."

something criminal. Another fear was that her server might be less secure than the government servers, leaving her open to being hacked—an event that would be disastrous if any of the emails discussed top-secret government information. In fact, a lawsuit was filed against Clinton, claiming that the reduced security of her emails "led to the deaths of two of the Americans killed in the 2012 attack on the U.S. diplomatic compound in Benghazi, Libya."[22] However, a federal judge dismissed the lawsuit, saying there was no evidence of this claim.

When Clinton's emails were examined, it was found that few of them discussed government secrets; of the 7,000 emails released, only 125 were made classified, or secret, by the State Department. Clinton insisted she had never discussed anything that was classified at the time. Additionally, she did not break any laws; there is a law that requires government officials to move their private emails onto government servers, but it was not put in place until 2014, after Clinton was no longer the secretary of state. The State Department confirmed her claim that she had not sent or received information that was classified at the time. The Justice Department did launch an inquiry, or investigation, into the email issue, but it stated that it was not to see whether Clinton had broken any laws; instead, it was to determine how classified information was handled.

Hillary Clinton's emails have been the focus of debate for several years.

Despite being cleared of wrongdoing by the government investigations against her, Clinton's emails remained a major focus, especially in the 2016 presidential campaign. She was given the nickname "Crooked Hillary" by her opponents, and people at political rallies—especially those in support of her presidential opponent, Donald Trump—often started chants of "Lock her up," even though the Justice Department had stated she had not broken any laws. Many of her opponents believed people in the government were covering up for Clinton and that she had actually been involved in some kind of illegal activity, so the Justice Department's statements did not convince them. Eleven days before the election, James Comey, the director of the Federal Bureau of Investigation (FBI) at the time, announced that the FBI was reviewing more of Clinton's emails. Clinton and her supporters placed some of the blame for her loss of the presidency on this announcement, which renewed people's suspicions that she had acted illegally. Others disagree with this claim, saying there were more problems with Clinton than just her emails.

In January 2018, the email issue was revisited yet again. The Justice Department began looking for answers to questions such as "how much classified information was sent over Clinton's server; who put that information into an unclassified environment, and how; and which investigators knew about these matters and when."[23] President Trump has continued to state that he is one of the people who does not believe Clinton did not do anything illegal.

Corruption and Donald Trump

Trump has had to deal with his own allegations of corruption. Officials in his campaign and his administration have faced accusations of collusion with foreign governments, while members of the president's family have faced criticism for involvement in business dealings with foreign nations while associated with the U.S. government. Early on, Trump faced criticism when he refused to divest himself of his business holdings, as previous presidents have. This means he chose not to sell any of the businesses he owns, although he did resign from all positions he held in which he had a direct say in the business. His two oldest sons took control over the businesses, "an arrangement that watchdogs said would not prevent conflicts of interest in the White House."[24] Experts are concerned Trump may make presidential decisions that benefit him financially, although Trump has promised not to do that. If he had sold his businesses, this would not be possible. The president is not required to divest his business interests, but it is widely regarded by political experts—including the U.S. Office of Government Ethics—as a good idea so the president can avoid accusations of fraud and corruption.

Another accusation Trump faced was that he had colluded with Russia during the 2016 election. There is evidence to suggest that Russia influenced the election to help Trump win, but experts disagree on how influential Russia was as well as whether or not Trump knew what the Russian government was doing. As of early 2018, an investigation is ongoing into this issue because when a foreign government spends money to influence a U.S. election, it could be a crime, especially if a U.S. citizen worked with the foreign government. The investigation was set up to look at how much influence Russia had and whether the Trump campaign worked with the Kremlin (a term for the Russian government).

According to testimony by Facebook executives, the Kremlin may have helped create as many as 80,000 fake news and propaganda (misleading information used to promote a certain political cause or point of view) posts, which were seen by more than 29 million Americans. These posts included ads that made Clinton seem bad and Trump seem good, and some of the information in them was proven to be false. One ad aimed to keep people away from the polls by telling them their vote would count if they simply tweeted it with the hashtag #PresidentialElection. The ad was Photoshopped onto a picture of popular actor, author, and comedian Aziz Ansari—someone

The relationship between the Trump administration and Russia, led by Vladimir Putin, has been the subject of investigation.

people might be likely to trust. The information, however, was false; social media posts are never counted as legitimate votes, and trying to trick people into not voting is called voter suppression, which is a federal crime. Russian sources created thousands of Twitter, Facebook, and other social media accounts to spread this kind of fake news. Whether or not the Trump administration knew about these ads or participated with the Kremlin has yet to be determined.

Although the charges have been denied by the administration, evidence has surfaced that at least some administration members did commit crimes, and others may have known about it. In November 2017, former national security adviser Michael Flynn was charged with lying to the FBI about conversations he had had with a Russian diplomat by Robert Mueller, who was appointed by the Justice Department to investigate the scandal. According to *Wired* magazine, Mueller's investigation has been focused on five specific areas as of early 2018: business deals and money laundering connected to Trump campaign staff; the extent of Russia's interference in the U.S. election; whether the Russians hacked political targets such as the DNC; whether the Russians met with campaign staff to discuss deals; and whether Trump is guilty of obstruction of justice by trying to stop the investigation.

Flynn had a close relationship with Trump, which made experts suspect that Trump was aware of what Flynn had been doing. Specifically, Flynn was accused of discussing U.S. sanctions against Russia with Sergey Kislyak, who was a Russian ambassador to the United States at the time of the presidential campaign. "Sanctions" refers to a policy of withdrawing trade partnerships as punishment for violating international codes. Because Russia invaded Ukraine without first being attacked, the United States passed laws stating that "[n]o U.S. oil company can do business with Russia, nor can any companies sell drilling technology needed to access oil and gas reserves. U.S. banks cannot issue long-term loans to Russian businesses for energy-focused projects."[25] Flynn denied these accusations repeatedly, but officials eventually found evidence that Flynn had been talking to Kislyak about removing these sanctions; some believe this is because Trump's businesses would make a bigger profit if he could do business with Russia. Since he has not divested himself from the businesses, this has made him the target of suspicion.

Another action that cast suspicion onto Trump was when he fired FBI director James Comey in May 2017. The official reason given by the White House was that the FBI staff had lost confidence in Comey due to the way he handled the investigation into Clinton's emails; however, this was contradicted by Andrew McCabe, who took over after Comey's dismissal but was fired in early 2018. Comey later announced that he believed he was fired because Trump had asked him to stop investigating Flynn. This was denied by the White House, but in a meeting with Russian officials, Trump said, "I just fired the head of the FBI … I faced great pressure because of Russia. That's taken off."[26] When asked by NBC why he had fired Comey, Trump did not mention the email investigation; instead, he said, "I said to myself, I said, 'You know, this Russia thing with Trump and Russia is a made-up story,'"[27] implying that he had fired Comey for not dropping the investigation into Flynn. The scandal and accusations of corruption has prompted some members of Congress—both Democrats and Republicans—to call for Trump's impeachment, although experts say this is unlikely to happen due to the difficulty involved in impeaching a president.

As of March 2018, Mueller's investigation is still ongoing, but a separate investigation by the House Intelligence Committee, headed by Republican K. Michael Conaway, found no evidence of collusion. Some people, especially Democratic members of the committee, have criticized this, saying the report should not have been issued until Mueller finished his investigation and accusing Republicans of covering up for Trump, who is also a Republican. Republicans have denied these accusations, saying their investigation was thorough enough to remove any suspicion of collusion. Some Democrats have expressed a desire to reopen the investigation at a later time, and Mueller's report has yet to be issued, so as of early 2018, the final outcome is not conclusive.

PAYING FOR POLITICS?

"The problem ... [is] who pays for politics. Elected officials ... [cannot] avoid the lobbyists who control, directly or indirectly, much of the money that pays for elections."
–Mark Schmitt, director of political reform programs at the New America Foundation, a non-partisan public policy research group

Mark Schmitt, "The Limits of Limits," American Prospect, March 2, 2007. prospect.org/article/limits-limits.

Corruption at All Levels of Government

Corruption can be found in lower government offices as well as in the highest offices. For instance, in the 1990s, a congressional post office scandal revealed a scheme to launder money from the U.S. post office, which led to the indictment of Democratic House Ways and Means Committee chairman Dan Rostenkowski on corruption charges. Rostenkowski was charged with keeping nonexistent employees on his payroll, using congressional funds to buy gifts for friends, and trading in officially purchased stamps for cash at the House post office.

Each decade seems to bring with it new instances of corruption in Congress. The corruption scandals that resulted in the indictment and resignation of Republican House majority leader Tom DeLay for campaign finance violations and Randy "Duke" Cunningham for outright bribery are just two examples. Former Republican Senate majority leader Bill Frist, too, was linked with numerous ethical and financial trading violations, and Republican congressman Bob Ney pleaded guilty to conspiracy charges in the Abramoff corruption investigation.

Senator Robert Menendez was found guilty of bribery and fraud.

In 2015, Senator Robert Menendez was indicted on charges of conspiracy, bribery, and fraud for accepting $1 million in gifts from a New Jersey businessman. In exchange, Menendez used his power in the Senate to benefit the businessman's personal and financial interests. Just one year later, Pennsylvania Democrat Chaka Fattah was found guilty of twenty-three charges of corruption that included fraud, money laundering, and racketeering.

A ROTTEN SYSTEM

"Nothing in the relationship of Enron to the Bush administration or to government regulators has yet been found to have been illegal. Enron simply provides another demonstration of the role of corporate money in the American system. It is the system that is rotten."
—William Pfaff, journalist

William Pfaff, "The American Problem Is Domination of Politics by Money," *International Herald Tribune*, January 24, 2002. archive.commondreams.org/scriptfiles/views02/0124-01.htm.

When Corporate Money Goes Wrong

Some of the nation's most serious corruption scandals have involved major U.S. corporations and their lobbyists. These scandals show how much influence corporate money has on government policies and the negative consequences it often has on the public good. One historic example is the 1980s savings and loan scandal. Savings and loan businesses traditionally had served as community-based businesses that provided home loans. In 1982, President Reagan signed legislation that removed savings and loans from federal regulation and allowed them to expand into speculative investments and loans that they knew little about. Reagan policy makers and Congress then looked the other way, allowing these businesses to make risky investments and misspend depositors' savings while the politicians accepted millions in campaign contributions from the wealthy owners. By the late 1980s, almost a quarter of these savings and loan businesses failed and the entire industry collapsed, creating a large financial scandal.

Charles Keating is a name that is synonymous with the savings and loan corruption scandal. Keating, the head of a savings and loan

Sting Operation

The FBI is the federal agency that investigates political corruption. In fact, the FBI's website states that corruption is one of the agency's top priorities. One of the FBI's most famous corruption investigations occurred in 1978, when an FBI sting operation called ABSCAM targeted members of Congress who were suspected of political corruption. A sting operation is when law enforcement officials trick criminals into revealing themselves. In ABSCAM, FBI employees posed as Middle Eastern businessmen and offered money to legislators in return for political favors to a nonexistent sheik (Middle Eastern leader). Altogether, six federal legislators—one senator and five members of the House of Representatives—were convicted of bribery and conspiracy. Also, one House member was convicted of a lesser charge, and a dozen lesser government officials received criminal sentences.

Representative Michael Myers (second from left) was caught on tape accepting money from an undercover FBI agent. He was the first House member to be expelled from Congress in more than 120 years.

business in California, convinced his customers to invest in worthless junk bonds. He was convicted of fraud, racketeering, and conspiracy in 1993 and sent to prison. Five U.S. senators were also implicated. Three of them were found to have assisted Keating by meeting with regulators who were investigating his business dealings in exchange for a total of $1.3 million in campaign contributions. The scandal brought wealth to a few people, but at a terrible public price: U.S. taxpayers had to pay more than $125 billion to cover the industry's federally insured accounts.

In the mid-2000s, the George W. Bush administration's close ties to Enron, a Texas energy company, dominated headlines and sparked widespread public criticism and anger. From its founding in 1985 until it grew into America's seventh-largest company, Enron had been a major supporter and friend of the entire Bush family. As Kevin Phillips explained,

> *It seems clear, counting campaign contributions, consultancies, joint investments, deals, presidential library and inaugural contributions, speech fees and the like, that the Bush family and entourage collected some $8 million to $10 million from Enron over the years ... Depending on some still-unclear relationships, it could be as high as $25 million.*[28]

This support positioned Enron to be close to both Bush presidents, and the company's influence was present at the top levels of decision-making.

When George W. Bush began his presidency in 2001, he appointed dozens of Enron officials, advisers, and consultants to high-level positions within the new administration. The energy sector was of particular interest to Enron; officials were especially involved in energy policy, meeting numerous times with Vice President Dick Cheney and his energy task force. Recommendations made by Enron in an April 2001 memo to Cheney, for example, became part of the administration's energy plan. As journalist John Nichols explained,

> *Seventeen policies sought by Enron or that clearly benefit[ed] the company—including proposals to extend federal control of transmission lines, use federal eminent-domain authority to override state decisions on transmission-line siting, expedite [speed up] permitting for new energy facilities and limit the use of price controls—were included.*[29]

Enron and the Bush administration maintained close ties throughout a California energy crisis from 2000 to 2001. The crisis caused huge jumps in the price of electricity and numerous rolling blackouts for millions of American consumers. Despite widespread calls for intervention during the crisis, the administration refused to investigate complaints about market manipulation by energy companies. Later, evidence clearly showed that Enron had manipulated the market with price-fixing schemes to profit from the California crisis.

Representative Henry Waxman, a Democratic member of the House Committee on Government Reform, began an investigation in 2003 into Enron's influence with the Bush administration and questioned what he called "the administration's failure to take prompt and effective action to protect Western consumers from price gouging and market manipulation."[30] Vice President Cheney, however, refused to turn over the records of his task force or meetings with Enron representatives, and the administration stonewalled the investigation.

When Enron imploded in December 2001, Bush refused to help the company with a federal bailout. However, Bush may have aided the company by easing government regulations, allowing the energy company to undertake speculative business ventures that led to massive fraud. As journalist Sam Parry said,

A woman is shown here protesting Dick Cheney's involvement with Enron outside of a Republican Party fund-raiser in 2002.

Bush pitched in as governor and president whenever the energy trader wanted easier regulations within the U.S. or to have U.S. taxpayers foot the bill for loan guarantees or risk insurance for Enron's overseas ventures ...

Enron wouldn't have ... [been] in a position for its executives to make off with hundreds of millions of dollars while leaving small investors and low-level employees to take the fall—without years of assistance from George W. Bush.[31]

Corruption scandals such as these have caused many to believe that America's top elected officials have not worked for the good of the people in a long time. Instead, they are doing the bidding of their wealthy and corporate donors. As journalist Bill Moyers argued,

Look back at legislation passed by Congress ... an energy bill that gives oil companies huge tax breaks at the same time that ExxonMobil ... posted $36.13 billion in profits and our gasoline and home heating bills [were] at an all-time high; a bankruptcy "reform" bill written by credit card companies to make it harder for poor debtors to escape the burdens of divorce or medical catastrophe; the deregulation of the banking, securities and insurance sectors, which brought on rampant corporate malfeasance [wrongdoing] and greed and the destruction of the retirement plans of millions of small investors; the deregulation of the telecommunications sector, which led to cable industry price-gouging and an undermining of news coverage; protection for rampant overpricing of pharmaceutical drugs; and the blocking of even the mildest attempt to prevent American corporations from dodging an estimated $50 billion in annual taxes by opening a P.O. box in an off-shore tax haven like the Cayman Islands.[32]

Despite its status as the largest and most open democracy in the world, the United States is still stuck in corruption, much of it driven by the enormous amounts of money flowing into its election system.

CHAPTER 4

A Global Problem

The reality of political corruption in the United States is problematic, but in some other countries, corruption is openly practiced; people in those countries are aware that they are expected to bribe police or government officials in routine dealings with them. The website Life Remotely published a book for tourists who travel to Mexico and Central America which explained the most common form of bribery they are likely to encounter:

> Bribe shakedowns typically start after you've been stopped for a bogus infraction [fake offense]. The cop will tell you what you have to do to pay the (usually outrageous) fine. This often involves driving an hour in the wrong direction to a police station. As soon as you decline, he'll offer a cheaper alternative, cash in his hand.[33]

In developing countries, the absence of basic anti-corruption laws allows such corruption to flourish. However, industrialized, democratic countries such as the United States also face high levels of corruption; it is simply more hidden. As economics scholar Robert Klitgaard explained, "Corruption exists everywhere, in private as well as public sectors, in rich countries and poor."[34] As the world moves increasingly toward globalization, with it comes a rise in corruption at the international level.

Activists took to the streets of Amsterdam, the Netherlands, in November 2017 to protest government corruption.

WIDESPREAD DAMAGE

"The true impact of corruption is now widely acknowledged: corruption distorts markets and competition, breeds cynicism among citizens, undermines the rule of law, damages government legitimacy, and corrodes the integrity of the private sector. It is also a major barrier to international development—systemic misappropriation by kleptocratic governments harms the poor."
—Ben W. Heineman Jr., senior fellow at Harvard's Belfer Center for Science and International Affairs, and Fritz Heimann, cofounder of Transparency International

Ben W. Heineman Jr. and Fritz Heimann, "The Long War Against Corruption," Foreign Affairs, May/June 2006. www.foreignaffairs.com/articles/2006-05-01/long-war-against-corruption.

Where in the World Is There Corruption?

Each year, TI publishes a Corruption Perception Index, which ranks countries based on the level of corruption found there in the previous year. The lowest-ranked countries suffer from badly functioning public services, collusion between governments, misappropriation of funds, and more. In the most corrupt countries in the world, the citizens face high levels of poverty, political instability, few political freedoms, and weak legal and financial institutions—characteristics that typically define poorer, developing nations. In TI's 2018 list, 8 of the top 10 most corrupt nations are in Africa. Other poor and less developed regions, however, such as certain parts of China, Latin America, and Eastern Europe, have also seen high levels of corruption. Scandinavian countries such as Denmark, Finland, Sweden, and Norway, along with New Zealand, Switzerland, Singapore, the Netherlands, Luxembourg, and Canada top the list as the 10 least corrupt countries, but the organization notes that none of these countries came close to earning a perfect score.

Developing countries with large oil industries have traditionally been some of the most prone to corruption. As TI chairman Peter Eigen explained in 2004,

> Oil-rich Angola, Azerbaijan, Chad, Ecuador, Indonesia, Iran, Iraq, Kazakhstan, Libya, Nigeria, Russia, Sudan, Venezuela and Yemen all have extremely low scores. In these countries, public contracting in the oil sector is plagued by revenues vanishing into the pockets of Western oil executives, middlemen and local officials.[35]

Although some of these countries' scores have improved since then, many experts agree that the presence of valuable natural resources such as oil generally makes life worse for people in developing countries, not better. Battles over these valuable resources often lead to greater political instability and conflict, dictatorial or unrepresentative government, and widespread corruption.

Corruption in developing nations typically involves openly corrupt actions by high-level government officials. In fact, kickbacks on government contracts are commonplace in these places, and many presidents have been accused of embezzling millions or even billions of public funds from their countries. The poorest and most vulnerable citizens pay the biggest price for corruption because such practices divert scarce government resources away from legitimate public needs, such as social programs, education, and health care. This, in turn, often results in the continuation of poverty and disease as well as ineffective, repressive governments that only benefit a wealthy few.

Because corruption has a negative effect on a country's economy, leaders of organizations such as the International Monetary Fund (IMF) and United Nations Economic Commission for Africa (ECA) are interested in finding ways to fight it.

The economies of developing nations also suffer the effects of corruption. According to international agencies such as the World Bank and the IMF, corruption in weak economies reduces international developmental aid and slows economic growth by scaring away investors and donors, who worry that their money will go missing. In a mid-1990s World Bank survey, representatives from more than 60 developing nations agreed that corruption was the main obstacle to economic development and growth. Economist Shang-Jin Wei explained,

> For international investors, having to pay bribes and deal with official extortion is equivalent to facing an extra tax. Some foreign firms may have obtained business because of the bribes they paid. But for every dollar of business that these firms obtain, the country loses multiple dollars of potential foreign investment. My research estimates that an increase in the host country corruption from a low level such as that in Singapore to a higher level, such as that in Mexico, has the same negative effect on inward foreign direct investment (FDI) as raising the corporate tax rate by fifty percentage points. This negative impact is akin [similar] to a tax on firms in that it discourages investment. But, unlike a tax, corruption generates no tax revenue for the government.[36]

In Latin America, for example, corruption has long been widespread and is seen as a major cause of the region's slow economic growth and persistent poverty. Latin American democracies created after several bitter civil wars in the 1980s have, in recent years, been threatened by a host of corruption scandals involving high-level officials. For instance, Honduran former president Rafael Callejas was suspected and later acquitted (found innocent) of misappropriating government funds, but pled guilty in a bribery scandal involving the world soccer, or football, organization Féderation Internationale de Football Association (FIFA) in 2015. Officials found evidence that wealthy governments were bribing FIFA to hold the World Cup in their country. This had the effect of making rich countries richer while hurting poorer countries. According to the BBC,

> The World Cup is the most-watched sporting event in the world, larger even than the Olympics. It generates billions of dollars in revenue from corporate sponsors, broadcasting rights and merchandising. These arrests and investigations cast doubt over the transparency and

honesty for the process of allocating World Cup tournaments ... and the administration of funds, including those earmarked for improving football facilities in some of Fifa's poorer members.[37]

In South America, Venezuela under the presidency of Nicolás Maduro is considered one of the most corrupt countries in the world. Maduro became the president of Venezuela in 2013. His administration's mismanagement of social policies led Venezuela into a severe economic depression that caused crime, poverty, food shortages, and inflation to rise—and public discontent with it. Maduro has been accused of leading with authoritarian rule and trying to have the country's constitution rewritten to increase his power; Venezuelans have protested, and many have been killed for doing so. At the end of 2017, Venezuela was facing financial crisis as the fear of its state-run companies defaulting on their loans seemed close to becoming a reality.

Venezuelan president Nicolás Maduro has been called one of the world's most corrupt leaders.

Often, government corruption becomes closely linked with criminal activity. In many formerly Communist parts of eastern and southern Europe, for example, the breakdown of communism in the late 1980s caused a scramble for power and government assets that has resulted in a wave of crime and corruption.

Such is the case in Bosnia, where power struggles and ethnic tensions resulted in a war that began in 1992. During the war, gangs developed, black markets sold illegal goods, and criminals managed to loot much of the country's wealth as well as the aid that poured in from other countries. A 1995 peace accord ended the fighting, but crime and corruption persisted and made Bosnia's recovery from war very difficult. As TI spokesperson Srdjan Blagovcanin explained, "The reason for the stagnation of the fight against corruption in Bosnia is ties of the political elite with organized crime ... It is not a secret in Bosnia that a very big number of politicians have very close connections with people from the other side of the law."[38]

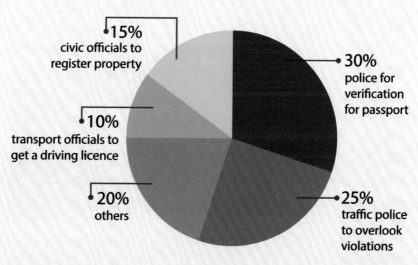

Who Do Indians Bribe the Most?

- 15% civic officials to register property
- 10% transport officials to get a driving licence
- 20% others
- 30% police for verification for passport
- 25% traffic police to overlook violations

This information from India Today *magazine shows that bribery is a normal part of life in India and is often required in routine transactions. This extra cost places a burden on citizens.*

Developed but Not Safe from Corruption

Even the world's most developed nations continue to struggle with the problem of corruption. The economic effects may be less severe in richer countries than in poorer countries, but corruption still acts as a dangerous negative force that threatens

Mexico's History of Corruption

Mexico has many advantages, such as oil, agriculture, and tourism, that could make it a very prosperous country, but it fails to succeed largely because of a long history of government corruption. In fact, corruption is so widespread in Mexico that it takes a bribe to government officials to do just about anything—open a business, obtain a driver's license, or apply for public services. Corruption essentially acts as a hidden tax that slows the country's economic growth.

The Mexican Institute for Competitiveness reported that corruption causes a 10 percent loss in the country's gross domestic product (GDP), which is the total amount of money the country makes in a year; eliminates almost half a million jobs annually; and reduces foreign investment by 5 percent. However, the most serious consequence is the suppression of the Mexican people's civil, social, economic, and political rights. As of 2018, Mexico is ranked 135th (out of 180) on TI's Corruption Perception Index. While corruption in Mexico has a longstanding history, it has become worse in recent years.

Shown here are activists assembling outside the attorney general's office in Mexico City in 2017, protesting government spying and demanding an end to corruption.

government stability and people's well-being. As Kimberly Ann Elliott explained,

> Even in rich countries diverted resources will not be available for improving living standards. Corruption also tends to exacerbate income inequalities by increasing the power of those willing and able to pay bribes to the detriment of those who cannot ... Finally, corruption can undermine political legitimacy in industrialized democracies as well as in developing ones by alienating the citizenry from its political leadership and making effective government more difficult.[39]

A number of European democracies have faced major scandals in recent decades. France, for example, has been plagued by a string of political scandals that have involved illegal political fund-raising by some of its most elite leaders. One of the most notorious French political scandals was called the Clearstream affair, and it has been compared to the American Watergate scandal. It began with an investigation of possible kickbacks associated with the 1991 sale of six French warships to Taiwan. In 2004, judges investigating the matter received an anonymous list of foreign bank accounts linked to various politicians, including Nicolas Sarkozy, France's interior minister and presidential candidate. The list itself, however, was found to be fake, and later evidence from a retired government spy has suggested that then-Prime Minister Dominique de Villepin and President Jacques Chirac may have created the list as part of a political smear campaign against Sarkozy to keep him from winning the election. Sarkozy did become the president of France, but he had his fair share of political scandals—including accusations of illegal campaign funding activity, attempts to influence judges, and false accounting—that caused him to fall out of favor with the French people.

MAKING BAD PROBLEMS WORSE

"In poor countries, corruption may lower economic growth, impede economic development, and undermine political legitimacy, consequences that in turn exacerbate [make worse] poverty and political instability."
–Kimberly Ann Elliott, visiting fellow at the Center for Global Development

Kimberly Ann Elliott, ed., *Corruption and the Global Economy.* Washington, DC: Institute for International Economics, 1997, p. 1.

In England, an expenses scandal became public in 2009. Members of Parliament (MPs) were found to have been claiming personal expenses for work, which allowed them to be paid for things such as renovating their homes and taking vacations. In 2017, the scandal was renewed when the Independent Parliamentary Standards Authority (IPSA), a group that was formed in 2009 to oversee MPs' expenses, was the victim of a data breach. The names, salaries, and bonuses of every MP's staff were accidentally published online; this information showed that many MPs were employing family members and paying them huge amounts of taxpayer money.

Even Germany, one of the least corrupt countries on TI's Corruption Perception Index, has faced serious corruption problems. In one 1993 scandal, for example, Premier Werner Munch, then head of the eastern state of Saxony-Anhalt, resigned after he and three of his ministers were found to have taken about $600,000 in undisclosed income from the government.

Notably, many of the corruption scandals in European countries have involved campaign finance motivations, the same type of corruption problem that is systemic in U.S. politics. Some commentators attribute this to the fact that European elections are becoming more Americanized—that is, focused primarily on personalities and appearances rather than on issues and

Targeting Infrastructure

Experts say global corruption is especially damaging in the construction sector. TI led a study in which it found that when bribes and other forms of corruption infect large-scale public infrastructure projects such as roads, bridges, and rail lines, the resulting projects are often overpriced, badly constructed, and built in areas that can damage the environment or even cost human lives. As TI chairman Peter Eigen explained,

Corrupt contracting processes leave developing countries saddled with sub-standard infrastructure and excessive debt ... Corruption raises the cost and lowers the quality of infrastructure. But the cost of corruption is also felt in lost lives. The damage caused by natural disasters such as earthquakes is magnified in places where inspectors have been bribed to ignore building and planning regulations ... Corruption can also have disastrous environmental consequences.[1]

1. Quoted in "A World Built on Bribes? Corruption in Construction Bankrupts Countries and Costs Lives, Says TI Report," Transparency International, accessed on February 23, 2018. www.transparency.org/news/pressrelease/a_world_built_on_bribes_corruption_in_construction_bankrupts_countries_and.

requiring ever-larger amounts of campaign money for expensive television ad campaigns.

Another theory is that Europe is a target for graft, patronage, and other forms of corruption because of its large social welfare system and the large number of political appointees. Others blame modern economic trends. Privatization, for example, encourages governments to contract with private companies for the provision of public services or utilities. Critics say this encourages bribery from companies competing to win these high-paying deals and can lead to situations in which government officials can hand out or influence hiring for high-paying jobs in these companies, but without the close examination that would come if the jobs were with the government.

Nicolas Sarkozy fell out of favor with many French citizens after he was accused of several forms of corruption. This protestor holds a sign reading "Sarkozy reform."

The Importance of Voting

Regardless of the motivation, corruption is causing disillusionment and cynicism about politics, even in some of the world's strongest democracies. In some cases, this takes the form of voters voting out the political party in power in favor of the opposition. In some countries, public disgust over corruption scandals has resulted in protest votes for fringe candidates.

In the United States, where there are only two main political parties, public apathy has increasingly led to low voter turnout.

The 1996 U.S. presidential election, for example, produced the lowest voter turnout since 1924, with only 49 percent of the voting-age population casting votes. The three most recent elections, in 2008, 2012, and 2016, have seen voter turnouts of around 60 percent. In the 2016 election, some people voted for third-party candidates such as Jill Stein of the Green Party. Although this may have reflected the voter's personal political views, third-party candidates generally do not get enough votes to win, so many people who voted third party were accused of "throwing away" their vote. Others disagree, noting that third party candidates will never have a chance if no one votes for them. However, some people who did not like any of the candidates protested by writing in candidates who had no chance of winning at all because they were not candidates, not real, not alive, or not human. Some of these write-ins included the Pope, Bill Nye the Science Guy,

In the 2016 U.S. presidential election, some voters expressed their frustration over their lack of choice in candidates by writing in silly options such as Abraham Lincoln (shown here).

a giant meteor, a cheese pizza, Harambe the gorilla, Bigfoot, Abraham Lincoln, and Mickey Mouse. One person wrote, "my dog, sincerely Tom H," while another wrote, "Anybody but the above!!!"[40] in reference to the names of those who were officially running. These write-in votes clearly show the frustration American voters feel with their limited choices, but without casting a legitimate vote, they have as little say in who wins as if they had not shown up to the polls at all.

Midterm congressional elections typically produce abysmally low voter turnouts, but the number of voters in the 1998 congressional elections dropped to a new low of only 38.1 percent of eligible voters—the lowest since 1942. Many people only turn up to vote in presidential elections, but experts say local and midterm elections are just as important, if not more so. Because of the American system of checks and balances, a president cannot fulfill all their campaign promises if they do not have support in Congress. This means that people who want to see certain policies passed need to vote for congressional candidates who will support those policies.

Voting may also be a way to reduce corruption because voting out politicians who are known to be corrupt allows more honest candidates to take office. However, some disagree with this view. According to *Smithsonian* magazine, the key to ending corruption is to fix the political system, which makes it easy for people to get away with corrupt behaviors: "As long as we see politics as a war between good and bad individuals, ignoring the structures that reward or punish them, this will continue."[41]

Increasing Opportunities for Corruption

The recent trend of globalization and increased trade brought on by advances in technology has only made countries and corporations more vulnerable to corruption. Today, large multinational corporations frequently trade with foreign governments or companies around the world, often in places where corruption is deeply rooted. To gain contracts with these countries, corporations based in richer nations have routinely bribed foreign leaders and officials of developing countries, even though such practices are prohibited. At the same time, illegal funds are becoming difficult to track and much easier to launder. Embezzlers or bribe takers have perfected the art of electronically transferring large amounts of cash to secret accounts or legitimate businesses in other countries. The result has been an escalation of corruption beyond national borders.

Some experts hold rich countries responsible for this growing problem of global corruption. Indeed, although the United States has banned foreign bribery since the 1977 Foreign Corrupt Practices Act, a number of other industrialized countries that have historically regulated corruption at home have nevertheless permitted their corporations to offer bribes overseas. As corruption expert Susan Hawley explained, "Until recently, bribery was seen as a normal business practice. Many countries including France, Germany and the UK treated bribes as legitimate business expenses which could be claimed for tax deduction purposes."[42]

CORRUPTION DOES NOT CAUSE SUCCESS

"It is possible ... to find examples of places that have done well [economically] in spite of corruption, but hard to think of anywhere that has done well because of it!"
–Shang-Jin Wei, economist

Shan-Jin Wei, "Corruption in Developing Countries," Brookings Institution, March 12, 2003. www.brookings.edu/on-the-record/corruption-in-developing-countries/.

This system, experts say, allowed rich countries and their corporations to exploit developing nations more easily for their natural resources—such as deposits of oil, copper, gold, and diamonds—and gain large profits. At the same time, however, the system has served to keep corrupt rulers in power in poor countries and allowed them to embezzle billions of dollars of public money that otherwise could have been used for reducing poverty and other problems faced by people in those developing regions. In fact, according to Hawley, "These bribes are conservatively estimated to run to ... roughly the amount that the UN estimates is needed to eradicate global poverty."[43]

In addition to taking billions away from the poor, this phenomenon of global corruption has a destabilizing effect on the world economy and international political relations. Just as at the national level, corruption on a wider scale distorts the global economic system in ways that prevent trade and growth. As globalization experts Patrick Glynn, Stephen J. Kobrin, and Moisés Naím explained,

> *Widespread corruption threatens the very basis of an open, multilateral world economy. Multilateralism depends on trust and a belief that others will play by the rules. The tendency to cheat ... is a constant threat to the international economic system. Tolerance of corruption tilts the playing field—against firms (and countries) that will not or cannot engage in bribes and other corrupt practices. Corruption distorts competition and may reduce gains from free flows of trade and investment.*[44]

CHAPTER 5

Standing Up to Corruption

Decades of corruption both in the United States and abroad have led to feelings of apathy or cynicism that corruption will always be present in politics. In recent years, public outcry has only become louder as news of corruption scandals breaks around the world.

With the rise of technology and the ability to share news items instantly, the public now has increased access to the tools that help them stay informed—and speak up. The publicity surrounding recent national and international corruption scandals has helped inspire a wave of anti-corruption efforts around the world.

Today, a new generation of reform advocates is demanding change, calling for reforms in the way companies conduct business with foreign partners, and pushing for the adoption and enforcement of stricter anti-corruption laws and limits to campaign finance practices. Anti-corruption laws and treaties, however, are often difficult to achieve because of resistance to change from those in power. Nevertheless, advocates for reform are continuing their fight for anti-corruption action to reduce the influence of money in elections and government.

Shown here is an anti-corruption activist in Thailand.

NO ACTION, NO PROGRESS

"Nearly half of the world's nations are corrupt, and many of them aren't doing very much about it at all."
–David A. Andelman, journalist and author

David A. Andelman, "A Stewpot of Corruption," *Forbes*, February 2, 2006. www.forbes.com/2006/02/03/corrupt-nations-world-cx_daa_0206caphosp.html.

Free to Take a Stand

Today, people around the world are becoming more aware of the consequences of corruption when left unaddressed. As corruption experts Glynn, Kobrin, and Naím wrote,

> There have been … increases in corrupt activity in various countries. In some regions, systemic political change has weakened or destroyed social, political, and legal institutions, opening the way to new abuses. Elsewhere, political and economic liberalization has simply exposed corruption that was once hidden. But almost everywhere, we observe a marked decrease in the willingness of the public to tolerate corrupt practices by their political leaders and economic elites.[45]

Many experts argue that the end of the Cold War in 1991 brought on this new culture of awareness. During the Cold War—the standoff between the United States and the Soviet Union that lasted for much of the 20th century—the focus was largely on opposing communism. The United States and other Western democracies formed relationships with developing nations without really caring whether their governments were corrupt. Western governments, as economist Robert Neild explained,

> were motivated, in part at least, by the view … that the West's supplies of raw materials and oil were threatened by communist intrusion into Third World countries. A feeling of vulnerability was understandable. The Soviet Union … was largely self-sufficient … the West, in need of increasing supplies for its growing industrial production, depended heavily on imports from Third World countries.[46]

As a result, many corrupt dictators stayed in power for decades, backed by Western weapons and loans. After the fall of communism and the breakup of the Soviet Union in 1991, people felt free to challenge corrupt dictatorships and demand more open and honest governments.

The increase in international trade after the Cold War also contributed to the concerns about corruption. Because a large part of many countries' economies relies on foreign trade, corruption in one country can have an impact on many other countries even when the corruption does not seem directly related to international affairs. This makes international efforts to reduce corruption even more urgent.

Ideas for Reform

Corruption has become, over the last few decades, a truly global issue. Although international organizations such as the UN, the World Bank, and the IMF had ignored corruption for many years, their indifference was challenged in 1996 when James Wolfensohn, then the World Bank president, made a speech in which he described the "cancer of corruption"[47] and its effects on the global economy. Since then, international organizations have banded together to seek global solutions to corruption practices, such as bribery and extortion, that happen around the world, no matter how developed the countries are.

The World Bank, for example, adopted a comprehensive anti-corruption program in the 1990s that includes both prohibitions against bribery in World Bank–financed projects and assistance to governments to promote anti-corruption reforms. The bank also has an arm of its operation dedicated to investigating instances of corruption and fraud related to projects it funds. This unit, called the Integrity Vice Presidency, looks into allegations of corruption in countries to which it provides development loans. Since its creation, the department has investigated more than 2,000 corruption cases. Similar efforts are being undertaken at the IMF and other international lending agencies.

The World Bank has monitored the effectiveness of governments since 1996, and it ranks countries according to factors such as their anti-corruption efforts, the strength of their legal systems, and improvements to government accountability and press freedom. The data collected by this program shows that the efforts to fight corruption have yet to solve the problem completely. A few countries have made some progress, while others have actually regressed and become more corrupt. The levels of corruption in a vast majority of other developing nations have remained about the same in recent decades.

The Anti-Corruption Summit, held in London in 2016, brought together 43 countries to discuss ways to stop international corruption.

The first big achievement of the international reform movement, however, came in 1997 with the Convention on Combating Bribery of Foreign Public Officials, a treaty that prohibits the use of bribes by companies seeking to win contracts in foreign countries. The treaty was adopted by the Organisation for Economic Co-operation and Development (OECD), an international agency made up of representatives from 35 member countries that supports programs for trade and development. All 35 OECD countries signed and ratified the treaty, along with 8 non-OECD countries that participated voluntarily.

The treaty was developed based on a U.S. ban on foreign bribes that was included in the Foreign Corrupt Practices Act of 1977. At the time, other countries did not immediately follow America's lead because they saw it as unnecessary. Those countries, therefore, continued to allow bribes to guide dealings between their multinational corporations for foreign contracts, sometimes even allowing companies to take tax deductions for the bribes. This practice was addressed 20 years later through the OECD treaty, which finally got other developed nations to adopt a bribery ban. As with any anti-corruption law, however, it will only succeed if it is enforced. With this treaty in particular, enforcement is important because the countries involved are industrialized, developed nations that are home to most of the multinational corporations that deal in global trading.

Anti-corruption initiatives have also been adopted by three regional organizations—the Council of Europe, the Organization of American States, and the African Union. In addition, the Asian Development Bank launched an anti-corruption plan that was signed by 25 Asian countries. North Africa and the Middle East—regions of the world whose countries rank highly on corruption lists—are working toward similar programs. One of the most effective treaties that has passed to date is the UN Convention Against Corruption (UNCAC), a treaty adopted by the UN General Assembly in 2003. The treaty addresses the topic of corruption more broadly than the OECD, including provisions on international corruption, criminalization, asset recovery, and prevention methods. It also provides guidance on implementation. Also, unlike the OECD convention, UNCAC encompasses both industrialized and less developed countries, creating the possibility of a worldwide anti-corruption program. It is the world's only legally binding, universal anti-corruption document.

The UN has created an international effort to stop corruption.

A DISILLUSIONING REALITY

"The reality of fighting corruption ...
has been a disillusioning experience in
most of the developing world."
—Donald Greenlees, reporter

Donald Greenlees, "Anti-Corruption Fight Stalled," *International Herald Tribune*, May 31, 2006.

Fighting the Status Quo

Even in the most developed nations, anti-corruption efforts have faced numerous obstacles. Although the United States has fewer problems with outright bribery and other unhidden corruption than in the past, it still has a campaign finance system that some have described as "more loophole than law."[48] The most recent significant reform was introduced in 2002, with the passing of the Bipartisan Campaign Reform Act (BCRA). This act was designed to end the use of soft money for activity related to federal elections.

The BCRA (also called the McCain-Feingold Act after its Senate sponsors, Arizona Republican John McCain and Wisconsin Democrat Russ Feingold) also increased the limits for hard money. Individuals can now contribute $2,000 in primary elections and $2,000 in general elections for each individual candidate, up to a total of $37,500 over a two-year election cycle, as well as up to $25,000 to a national party and $10,000 each to state parties. Furthermore, BCRA provided that ads that refer to a federal candidate cannot be broadcast within 30 days of a primary and 60 days of an election. Much of this part of the act was overturned later by the U.S. Supreme Court.

It was not long, however, before wealthy donors and candidates figured out how to circumvent BCRA's soft money ban. This was done through the use of tax-exempt political organizations known as 527s, named after a provision of the U.S. tax code. These 527s function very similarly to PACs, except that they are not regulated by the FEC and are not limited in the amounts they can collect or spend for issue ads. The consequences of 527s were seen almost immediately, during the 2004 presidential race between George W. Bush and John Kerry. Billionaire

George Soros gave more than $23 million to left-leaning 527 groups such as the Media Fund and MoveOn.org, which ran ads criticizing President Bush. At the same time, a wealthy Houston, Texas, home builder, Bob Perry, contributed more than $8 million to Swift Boat Veterans for Truth, a group that disparaged Kerry's Vietnam War record with a series of controversial, negative TV ads. Legislation has been introduced in both the House and the Senate to regulate 527s and similar political groups, but as of 2018, no new law has been enacted.

LITTLE LIKELIHOOD OF CHANGE

"Congress won't change because it doesn't want to. Lawmakers like the perks of the sleazy inside-the-Beltway political culture—the private jets, the junkets, the ease with which they can line up contributions. And they're confident that if they posture long enough, the public and the media eventually will lose interest."
—*San Diego Union-Tribune*, a daily newspaper serving San Diego, California

"Reform Follies: Congress' Hollow Posturing Invites Cynicism," *San Diego Union-Tribune*, March 10, 2006.

Many critics attribute the general lack of reform to reluctance by incumbents from both parties to change a system that benefits them. By using the loopholes in the system, incumbents can amass huge sums of money that virtually guarantee their reelection. As former Brown University political science professor Darrell M. West put it, "Washington's dirty little secret about campaign finance is that the major players are happy with things as they are. Incumbents do very well under contemporary rules. In recent elections, more than 90 percent of the men and women who have sought re-election to Congress have won."[49]

Sadly, the U.S. public's view of politicians as naturally corrupt only helps ensure that things stay the same. As West argued, "The people have become so desensitized to allegations of financial misdeeds that they assume little can be done about the problem."[50]

The media often contributes to this inaction by focusing on sensational news stories, such as small-time bribery scandals, and then failing to explore the deeper problem of systemic campaign finance corruption.

Clean Money Initiatives

Maine and Arizona were the first two states to enact Clean Money initiatives to provide for public financing of state candidates. Maine voters approved the Maine Clean Election Act in 1996, and Arizona voters approved the Citizens Clean Elections Act in 1998. In both states, the legislation was passed through citizen referendums rather than by the state legislatures and was later upheld by the state supreme courts after legal challenges. After several elections under these systems, advocates say the results are very positive. Most legislators currently serving in these states (64 percent of the legislative candidates in Maine's 2016 election and 9 out of 11 statewide officeholders in Arizona), for example, opted to use and were elected with public funds. The Clean Money system also produced more candidates, including many more women and minority candidates than in the past; allowed candidates to spend much more of their time interacting with voters; and increased voter turnout. Also, in recent years, legislators in both states have reportedly voted to protect the environment more often than before, have lowered the cost of prescription drugs, and have passed balanced budgets. These votes, advocates say, are the result of governments that are more representative of the people than of special interest groups.

Seeking an (Im)Perfect Solution

Finding a perfect solution to the problem of campaign finance corruption, however, may not be possible. Most reform ideas center around one or more of just a few basic approaches—limiting campaign spending, limiting donations, disclosure of donations, providing public financing, or providing free TV time—many of which have proven flaws. Limiting campaign spending may be accused of being a violation of First Amendment free speech rights under *Buckley v. Valeo*. Legislative limits on donations and disclosure laws, as history has shown, tend to be easily avoided by corporate and special interests determined to retain their influence on politics. The two remaining concepts—public funding and free TV airtime—now appear to be gaining more support.

In fact, a grassroots movement has been gaining ground in America to push for a public funding approach. This movement, called "Clean Money" or "Clean Elections," began in Maine in 1996 and has since spread to other states. In September 2017, the California legislature passed the California DISCLOSE Act, a set of campaign finance disclosure rules. Legislation such as this differs somewhat from state to state, but each one embodies one simple idea: the importance of keeping campaign financing practices transparent and aboveboard, or open and honest.

Typically, the Clean Money laws weed out fringe candidates by providing that candidates wishing to receive public funding must be a nominee of a party recognized by the state. Fringe candidates are those who have little to no chance of winning votes. Some run because they feel none of the existing parties represent their interests; for instance, in 2005, activist Jimmy McMillan created the Rent Is Too Damn High Party. He ran for various offices in New York on a platform of reducing the price of rent in New York City. Other fringe candidates run as independents, either for fun or to call attention to certain issues. A man called Vermin Supreme has run for president several times as an act of performance art; one of his campaign promises is a free pony for every citizen. However, he knows he will never be elected and is not a serious candidate. Anyone who meets the Constitutional requirements is allowed to run for president if they pay the registration fee, which Supreme

Vermin Supreme has run for president several times. He is considered a fringe candidate because he is not expected to win, although some people do vote for him by writing him in on the ballot.

once "paid in $50 bills marked 'not to be used for bribing politicians.'"[51]

Candidates must qualify by collecting a set number of small individual contributions from voters in their district. If they qualify, their campaigns are fully funded by the public and they are not permitted to use their own personal money or accept any outside donations, whether from individuals, corporations, or PACs. Candidates who choose not to participate in the Clean Money system can raise money from private donors, but they must follow state campaign finance limits and disclosure laws. If a Clean Money candidate faces an opponent who has chosen not to participate in the system and instead has chosen to accept large private contributions, most laws provide a matching grant—up to a certain limit—to the publicly funded candidate. Extra funding is also often provided if the opposing candidate has the help of independent groups such as PACs and 527s.

Advocates of the Clean Money approach claim it will clean up campaign finance corruption and promote better, more responsive government. By providing public campaign funds, they say, the program encourages a wider variety of qualified candidates to run for office and eliminates some of the historical advantages held by incumbents. Additionally, since candidates are free of having to raise money for their campaigns, they are able to spend their campaign time discussing issues and interacting with voters. This leads to more issue-oriented elections and encourages the voters to become more engaged in the political process. Finally, advocates argue that candidates who are elected with Clean Money will be better public servants because they will not have to worry about fund-raising and will owe no favors to campaign contributors.

Some critics dislike public funding of

Many citizens have attended anti-corruption protests.

campaigns because they believe it forces taxpayers to make political donations. As political scientist John Samples argued,

> *Those who wish to support the candidates and causes favored by government financing may do so now; they need only send their check to the candidate or cause they favor. Government financing forces all taxpayers to financially support candidates they would not otherwise support, candidates whose views they may find repugnant [disgusting].*[52]

NOT AN EASY FIGHT

"Fighting corruption is not easy. Anti-corruption campaigns are more often limited to rhetoric [insincere discussion], and are only rarely sustained."
—Shang-Jin Wei, economist

Shang-Jin Wei, "Corruption and Globalization," Brookings Institution, April 30, 2001. www.brookings.edu/research/corruption-and-globalization/.

Finding Success Through Different Approaches

Other industrialized democratic countries also face similar dilemmas about how to limit the influence of corporate and special interest money on elections, but most do not experience anywhere near the level of spending that occurs in the United States. Some of their solutions are similar to U.S. election finance reforms, such as prohibiting corporations from contributing directly to campaigns. In addition, contribution limits and public disclosure of private donations similar to the U.S. requirements are common in most democracies.

However, many experts believe that other democracies have had more success with campaign finance reform because they have adopted reforms that so far have been rejected or remain untried in the United States. For one thing, countries such as Canada, France, New Zealand, and Great Britain place strict limits on the amounts candidates can spend on their campaigns—the type of spending limits ruled unconstitutional for America in *Buckley v. Valeo.* In Great Britain, for example, the spending limits are quite low and result in relatively inexpensive campaigns.

In addition to spending limits, most foreign democracies have also adopted two other important reforms not yet widely used in the United States—public funding of elections and free TV airtime for candidates. Virtually all the northern European countries have adopted both of these approaches in some form. Other countries embracing both public funding and free airtime include Canada, Australia, New Zealand, Israel, Argentina, Brazil, Costa Rica, and Mexico.

However, these approaches have not necessarily rooted out all political corruption. As in the United States, political scandals continue to occur all over the world despite the various anti-corruption laws. In the end, therefore, reducing corruption may come down mostly to political will and enforcement efforts.

Looking Ahead with Hope

In the United States, political corruption is as old as the country itself, and so are the attempts to stop it. Although the centuries of attempts to fight corruption—and the successes and failures along the way—demonstrate how difficult it is to curb corruption, the fight continues with every new generation of citizens, reformers, and anti-corruption organizations.

The success of these efforts depends significantly on how committed governments are to eradicating corruption completely. Such commitment requires the adoption of anti-corruption measures as well as the resources to enforce them. In addition to taking a hard line on corruption, governments around the world must think ahead and pass laws that prevent corruption and abuses of power from happening in the first place. They must also protect the people who

Through collective international efforts, societies around the world can act to stop corruption.

are brave enough to report it. This kind of action requires strong leadership, even in the face of resistance.

Now more than ever is the time for citizens to get involved. Researching candidates and their backgrounds is a good place to start. An educated and informed electorate increases the chances of the right candidates being elected—and holds officials accountable when they are in office. While this task is huge, there is a reason to continue the fight against corruption, and it starts with regular citizens making their voices heard. As Ben Heineman Jr. and Fritz Heimann put it, "Ultimately, the most potent [powerful] force for change is the idea that corruption is morally repugnant and inimical [damaging] to competition, globalization, the rule of law, international development, and the welfare of citizens around the world."[53]

NOTES

Chapter 1: Understanding Political Corruption

1. "Helping Countries Combat Corruption: The Role of the World Bank: Corruption and Economic Development," The World Bank Group, accessed on February 22, 2018. www1.worldbank.org/publicsector/anticorrupt/corruptn/cor02.htm.

2. Steven P. Lanza, "The Economics of Ethics: The Cost of Political Corruption," *Connecticut Economy Quarterly*, February 24, 2004. webshare.business.uconn.edu/ccea/studies/Cost-of-Political-Corruption.pdf.

3. Susan Rose-Ackerman, *Corruption and Government: Causes, Consequences, and Reform.* New York, NY: Cambridge University Press, 1999, p. 132.

4. Elizabeth Drew, *The Corruption of American Politics: What Went Wrong and Why.* New York, NY: Overlook, 1999, p. 64.

5. Yascha Mounk, "America Is Not a Democracy," *The Atlantic*, March 2018. www.theatlantic.com/magazine/archive/2018/03/america-is-not-a-democracy/550931/.

6. Mounk, "America Is Not a Democracy."

7. Shang-Jin Wei, "Corruption in Economic Development: Beneficial Grease, Minor Annoyance, or Major Obstacle?," World Bank. www.worldbank.org/wbi/governance/pdf/wei.pdf.

Chapter 2: A Culture of Corruption

8. Quoted in Nathan Miller, *Stealing from America: A History of Corruption from Jamestown to Reagan.* St. Paul, MN: Paragon House, 1992, p. 167.

9. Quoted in Steve Padilla, "In Politics, Money Talks—and Keeps Talking, Despite Reforms," *Los Angeles Times*, July 16, 2000. www.campaignfinancesite.org/history/reform3.html.

10. Miller, *Stealing from America*, p. 262.

11. Frank J. Sorauf, *Money in American Elections*. Glenview, IL: Scott, Foresman, 1988, p. 32.

12. Sorauf, *Money in American Elections*, pp. 34–35.

Chapter 3: The Role of Money

13. Mark Green, *Selling Out: How Big Corporate Money Buys Elections, Rams Through Legislation, and Betrays Our Democracy*. New York, NY: Regan, 2002, p. 4.

14. Green, *Selling Out*, p. 105.

15. David Jolly, "Are Members of Congress Becoming Telemarketers?," *60 Minutes*, CBS News, April 24, 2016. www.cbsnews.com/news/60-minutes-are-members-of-congress-becoming-telemarketers/.

16. Quoted in "Congressional Fundraising: Last Week Tonight with John Oliver (HBO)," YouTube video, 21:24, posted by LastWeekTonight, April 3, 2016. www.youtube.com/watch?v=Ylomy1Aw9Hk&t=1139s.

17. Quoted in "Congressional Fundraising," YouTube video, posted by LastWeekTonight.

18. Quoted in Mollie Dickenson, "John McCain: Straight Shooter?," *Consortium News*, 2000. www.consortiumnews.com/2000/012900b.html.

19. Miller, *Stealing from America*, p. 341.

20. Miller, *Stealing from America*, p. 341.

21. Eric Bradner, "Hillary Clinton's Email Controversy, Explained," CNN, October 28, 2016. www.cnn.com/2015/09/03/politics/hillary-clinton-email-controversy-explained-2016/index.html.

22. Josh Gerstein, "Suit Against Hillary Clinton Over Benghazi Deaths and Emails Is Dismissed," Politico, May 26, 2017. www.politico.com/blogs/under-the-radar/2017/05/26/hillary-clinton-benghazi-email-suits-dismissed-238880.

23. Betsy Woodruff, "Justice Department 'Looking Into' Hillary Clinton's Emails—Again," Daily Beast, January 4, 2018. www.thedailybeast.com/justice-department-looking-into-hillary-clintons-emails-again.

24. Andy Sullivan, Emily Stephenson, and Steve Holland, "Trump Says Won't Divest from His Business While President," Reuters, January 11, 2017. www.reuters.com/article/us-usa-trump-finance/trump-says-wont-divest-from-his-business-while-president-idUSKBN14V21I.

25. Terrell Jermaine Starr, "The American Sanctions Against Russia, Explained," Foxtrot Alpha, February 3, 2017. foxtrotalpha.jalopnik.com/the-american-sanctions-against-russia-explained-1791938454.

26. Quoted in "Stupid Watergate: Last Week Tonight with John Oliver (HBO)," YouTube video, 24:05, posted by LastWeekTonight, May 21, 2017. www.youtube.com/watch?v=FVFdsl29s_Q.

27. Quoted in Philip Bump, "Timeline: What We Know About Trump's Decision to Fire Comey," Washington Post, January 5, 2018. www.washingtonpost.com/news/politics/wp/2018/01/05/timeline-what-we-know-about-trumps-decision-to-fire-comey/?utm_term=.fefb29cf5fa8.

28. Kevin Phillips, "Dynasties," Nation, June 20, 2002. www.thenation.com/article/dynasties/.

29. John Nichols, "Enron: What Dick Cheney Knew," Nation, March 28, 2002. www.thenation.com/article/enron-what-dick-cheney-knew/.

30. Quoted in Tim Wheeler, "Enron Entangles Bush, Cheney," People's Weekly World, June 1, 2002. www.pww.org/article/view/1297/1/88/.

31. Sam Parry, "Bush and Ken Lay: Slip Slidin' Away," Consortium News, February 6, 2002. www.consortiumnews.com/2002/020 602a1.html.

32. WS Editors, "Let's Save Our Democracy by Getting Money Out of Politics," Washington Spectator, April 1, 2006. washingtonspectator.org/lets-save-our-democracy-by-getting-money-out-of-politics/.

Chapter 4: A Global Problem

33. Life Remotely, *Don't Go There. It's Not Safe. You'll Die. And Other More Rational Advice for Overlanding Mexico & Central America*. E-book, 2012, p. 134.

34. Robert Klitgaard, "International Cooperation Against Corruption," Internet Center for Corruption Research, November 1997. www.icgg.org/downloads/contribution02_klitgaard.pdf.

35. Quoted in "Corruption Perceptions Index 2004," Transparency International, accessed on February 23, 2018. www.transparency.org/research/cpi/cpi_2004/0.

36. Shang-Jin Wei, "Corruption and Globalization," Brookings Institution, April 30, 2001. www.brookings.edu/research/corruption-and-globalization/.

37. "Fifa Corruption Crisis: Key Questions Answered," BBC, December 21, 2015. www.bbc.com/news/world-europe-32897066.

38. Quoted in Tanja Subotic and Banja Luka, "'Nothing Can Be Done Without Corruption' in Bosnia," *Mail & Guardian Online*, January 2006. www.mg.co.za/articlePage.aspx?articleid=260107&area=/insight/insight international/.

39. Kimberly Ann Elliott, ed., *Corruption and the Global Economy*. Washington, DC: Institute for International Economics, 1997, pp. 1–2.

40. Quoted in Teresa Boeckel, "Who Received Write-In Votes for President?," *York Daily Record*, December 1, 2016. www.ydr.com/story/news/2016/12/01/who-received-write-votes-president/94694780/.

41. Jon Grinspan, "To Stop an Endless Cycle of Corruption, History Says Fix the System, Not the Politician," *Smithsonian*, October 27, 2015. www.smithsonianmag.com/smithsonian-institution/what-early-20th-century-muckraker-lincoln-steffens-might-offer-21st-century-voter-180957052/.

42. Susan Hawley, *Exporting Corruption: Privatisation, Multinationals and Bribery*. Dorset, UK: Corner House, June 2000. www.thecornerhouse.org.uk/pdf/briefing/19bribe.pdf.

43. Hawley, *Exporting Corruption*.

44. Patrick Glynn, Stephen J. Kobrin, and Moisés Naím, "The Globalization of Corruption," *Corruption and the Global Economy*, p. 13.

Chapter 5: Standing Up to Corruption

45. Glynn, Kobrin, and Naím, "The Globalization of Corruption," p. 9.

46. Robert Neild, *Public Corruption: The Dark Side of Social Evolution*. London, UK: Anthem Press, 2002, pp. 136–137.

47. Quoted in Mario Ritter, "The World Bank Fights the 'Cancer of Corruption,' " Voice of America, April 7, 2006. www.voanews.com/specialenglish/archive/2006-04/2006-04-07voa 2.cfm.

48. Quoted in United States House of Representatives, "Christopher Shays and Marty Meehan, Testimony Before the House Administration Committee On H.R. 417, the Bipartisan Campaign Finance Reform Act," June 29, 1999. www.house.gov/shays/reform/ 629test5.htm.

49. Darrell M. West, *Checkbook Democracy: How Money Corrupts Political Campaigns*. Boston, MA: Northeastern University Press, 2000, p. 167.

50. West, *Checkbook Democracy*, p. 170.

51. Lucy Sweeney, "Vermin Supreme 2016: Alternative US Presidential Candidate Promises Free Ponies for All," ABC (Australian Broadcasting Corporation), January 25, 2016. www.abc.net.au/news/2015-11-25/vermin-supreme-us-presidential-candidate-promises-free-ponies/6972628.

52. John Samples, ed., *Welfare for Politicians: Taxpayer Financing of Campaigns*. Washington, DC: Cato Institute, 2005, p. 17.

53. Ben W. Heineman Jr. and Fritz Heimann, "The Long War Against Corruption," *Foreign Affairs*, May/June 2006. www.foreignaffairs.com/articles/2006-05-01/long-war-against-corruption.

DISCUSSION QUESTIONS

Chapter 1: Understanding Political Corruption

1. What does the term political corruption mean, according to the definition used by international organizations?

2. What is the purpose of government, and how does corruption defy it?

3. What are some of the most common forms of corruption in developing countries? Which forms are more commonly seen in developed nations?

Chapter 2: A Culture of Corruption

1. Who were the Progressives, and what were their goals?

2. Why were the 1974 FECA amendments unsuccessful in stopping the flow of corporate money into elections?

3. What do the terms "bundling" and "soft money" mean?

Chapter 3: The Role of Money

1. Why are American presidential and congressional campaigns so expensive?

2. What impact do rising campaign costs have on the nature of political positions?

3. Describe some of the presidential, congressional, and corporate corruption scandals in recent American history. Which do you think is the worst?

Chapter 4: A Global Problem

1. What are some social consequences of political corruption in developing nations?

2. What effect has globalization had on corruption?

3. Why is voting important?

Chapter 5: Standing Up to Corruption

1. Why is there an increased focus on corruption today?

2. How have organizations such as the World Bank and the International Monetary Fund worked to combat political corruption internationally? How effective have they been so far?

3. How do the Clean Money and Clean Elections laws work to combat the problem of money in American elections?

ORGANIZATIONS TO CONTACT

The Brookings Institution
1775 Massachusetts Avenue NW
Washington, DC 20036
(202) 797-6000
www.brookings.edu

> The Brookings Institution is a private, nonprofit research organization that provides analysis and recommendations for policy makers on a wide range of public policy issues. Its website contains an informative category on U.S. politics and campaign finance reform, with links to a number of publications on the topic.

The Center for Responsive Politics (CRP)
1300 L Street NW, Suite 200
Washington, DC 20005-5635
(202) 857-0044
www.opensecrets.org

> The CRP is a nonpartisan, nonprofit research group that tracks money in politics and its effect on elections and public policy. The center conducts computer-based research on campaign finance issues for the news media, academics, activists, and the public at large. Its website is a comprehensive resource for data related to federal campaign financing activity.

Citizens for Responsibility and Ethics in Washington (CREW)

455 Massachusetts Avenue NW
Washington, DC 20001
(202) 408-5565
www.citizensforethics.org

> CREW is a legal advocacy group that works to reduce the influence of money in politics and uses litigation and public advocacy to expose corrupt activities. The CREW website contains information about corruption scandals and the group's various advocacy efforts.

Common Cause

805 15th Street NW, Suite 800
Washington, DC 20005
(202) 833-1200
www.commoncause.org

> Common Cause is a nonpartisan, nonprofit advocacy organization founded in 1970 to encourage citizen participation in democracy and to promote an honest, open, and accountable government. Its website contains a wealth of information about money in U.S. politics and anti-corruption reforms.

International Anti-Corruption Resource Center (IACRC)

Sidley Building, 1501 K Street NW, Suite 700
Washington, DC 20005
(202) 736-8069
iacrc.org

> IACRC is a Washington-based nonprofit organization that trains investigators, auditors, and project personnel on how to prevent and detect corruption schemes. By training law enforcement agencies to pursue and remove government officials who are engaged in various levels of fraud, the agency works to create a fair and transparent business climate around the world.

FOR MORE INFORMATION

Books

Burgen, Michael. *Voting and Elections*. London, UK: Raintree Press, 2013.

> This look at election processes around the world shows how campaigns work and the process by which leaders make their way into office. This book also answers questions such as, "Where does the concept of voting come from?," "How do political leaders convince people to vote for them?," and "Has corruption ever helped someone get into office?"

Chastain, Zachary. *Scandals and Glory: Politics in the 1800s*. Broomall, PA: Mason Crest Publishers, 2011.

> The author describes American politics during the 19th century, discussing campaigns, candidates, and voting practices. Chastain also examines scandals, such as buying votes, stuffing ballot boxes, and other incidents of greed and corruption.

Hunt, Jilly. *Leaders*. Chicago, IL: Heinemann Library, 2013.

> This book examines international political leaders and discusses why and how societies demand certain standards of conduct from their leader.

Lansford, Tom. *Corruption and Transparency*. Broomall, PA: Mason Crest, 2017.

> Lansford discusses corruption, why it is the greatest danger to democracy, and how transparency provides the best means to prevent corruption by ensuring that the decisions and actions of officials are easily understood.

Websites

Federal Election Commission
www.fec.gov

>Explore historical and current data about the campaign finance process in the United States.

Transparency International (TI)
www.transparency.org

>TI's website includes its corruption report as well as a step-by-step guide for young activists on how they can get involved and take action against corruption.

United Against Corruption
www.anticorruptionday.org/actagainstcorruption/index.html

>This United Nations campaign encourages people around the world to get involved in fighting corruption.

U.S. Department of State: U.S. Anti-Corruption Efforts
www.state.gov/anticorruption/index.htm

>Managed by the U.S. Department of State, this government resource provides information on what the U.S. government is doing to fight political corruption.

The World Bank: Combating Corruption
www.worldbank.org/en/topic/governance/brief/anti-corruption

>This resource provides information on The World Bank Group's efforts to build transparent and accountable institutions around the world through its anti-corruption programs.

INDEX

PICTURE CREDITS

ABOUT THE AUTHOR

Sarah Machajewski is a professional writer with an interest in history and cultural exploration. She began her writing career as an author of nonfiction, educational books for juvenile audiences and now writes for the higher education sector. She lives in Buffalo, New York, and is currently pursuing a master's degree in education.